24 FOOTPATH WALKS AROUND ST. ALBANS

BILL FR(

With notes on places of interest

PUBLISHED BY ST ALBANS AND DISTRICT FOOTPATHS SOCIETY
1988

Second Edition 1990
Reprinted 1991
Third Edition 1993
Reprinted 1997
Fourth Edition 2000

INTRODUCTION

The St. Albans and District Footpaths Society under the chairmanship of Mr. H. L. Knapp, first published a booklet 'Footpath Walks Around St. Albans' in 1971, later revised in 1982. Another booklet entitled 'Short Walks in St. Albans District' was published in 1978. Since the inception of the Society in 1967, walks continue to be well supported throughout the year. On average ten walks per month are arranged, and we continue to clear and waymark paths in an effort to keep them open.

Unfortunately in the parishes of St. Michaels, St. Stephens and London Colney, we have lost 10% of our paths due to severance by motorways. This together with housing and industrial developments has resulted in a pressing need for an updated version of these booklets.

This new version is written to enable walkers confidently to complete circular walks along definitive or permissive paths, all within easy reach of St. Albans. The descriptions are written in some detail, and should be particularly helpful to those who have recently moved into this area, or who may have done little walking in the past, and have only recently discovered its pleasures. Generally the walks are described in a clockwise sense, but the counter clockwise route makes an interesting variation which is well worth trying. The accompanying maps shows stiles, signposts and gates, also Public Houses for refreshment en route. The item numbers on each map are used in both the text and in the 'Places of Interest' at the back of the booklet, making cross reference easy. To reinforce the text, frequent compass directions are given. These will be useful when, for example, crossing a field where a hedge has been removed, and the path has not been reinstated after ploughing. The script and maps were correct at the time of writing, but changes can occur quickly, and landmarks do disappear. This Society accepts no responsibility for changes or errors.

The Society would be grateful for readers observations concerning obstructions, overgrowth or waymarking. The Footpaths Officer at St. Albans District Council should also be informed.

To support our endeavour to keep paths open, and to avoid further loss, I hope many more people will continue to walk our paths, and so find pleasure in what little remains to us of a very ancient heritage, namely our old tracks and paths.

Further information can be obtained from officers of this Society listed at the Public Library in St. Albans.

Bill Frost
21 Cuckmans Drive,
St. Albans, Herts. AL2 3AY.
October, 1988.

Based upon the 1987 Pathfinder 1:25000 Ordnance Survey map by permission of Ordnance Survey on behalf of the Controller of Her Majesty's Stationery Office © Crown Copyright MC 100017856

Extracts from the List of Buildings of Special Architectural or Historic Interest are reproduced with the permission of the Controller of Her Majesty's Stationery Office.

FOREWORD

COUNCILLOR MICHAEL MORRELL
THE MAYOR OF THE CITY AND DISTRICT OF ST. ALBANS

I am delighted to write the foreword of the Fourth Edition for 24 Footpath Walks around St Albans.

The opportunity to explore a still beautiful part of Hertfordshire despite ever increasing traffic is a vital part of life in the City and District. The Footpaths Society has over the last 30 years provided an invaluable guide to a leisure pursuit which can restore calm and sanity to an increasingly frenetic world.

You can buy the book and explore on your own or alternatively join the other 300 members of the Society and discover Hertfordshire's secrets in the company of experts. They run two or three walks each week, have an invigorating winter social programme and a Work Group which helps maintain paths, gates, signs and stiles.

I look forward to many walks with the Guide as my companion.

Michael Morrell

Mayor and President 1999/2000

PREFACE TO THE FOURTH EDITION

Since the first edition of this book, 12,000 copies have been bought, which is a good indication of the interest in our footpaths by local residents and visitors.

The countryside is always changing: farm buildings are used for other purposes; land may change from agriculture to leisure or mineral extraction; prominent features disappear and new ones are raised; names of buildings and places alter. Inevitably, a guide-book gradually becomes inaccurate.

A team of members, ably organised by Peter Lawrence, has checked and re-checked every one of the twenty-four walks leading to corrections of the text and maps. Thanks to all who took part in the project.

So now, in 2000, here is the new-look fourth edition which incorporates all the latest changes and is as up-to-date as possible. The routes are the popular ones enjoyed by users of the first three editions and the only significant change old hands will spot is that the southern part of walk 16 now goes anti-clockwise to make crossing the A414 safer.

The society hopes that thousands more readers will get much pleasure and healthy walking, using this book.

Brian Chapman, Chairman
St. Albans & District Footpaths Society

ACKNOWLEDGMENTS

My thanks go to all members of The Society who have assisted in the production of this booklet, by checking the script and maps and by suggesting improvements and changes where necessary. Thanks are also due to Mrs. M. Wynn-Ruffhead for the cover design, and sketches, to Mr. G. Bailey for assistance with the historical notes, and to Mr. P. Constable for the cover layout. My personal thanks last but not least go to Emily, my wife, for her patience and help throughout the writing and revision of this book.

Reference has been made to the 'List of Buildings of Special Architectural or Historical Interest' published by the Department of Environment.

MAPS

Further supporting detail is obtainable from Ordnance Survey maps available from bookshops. The relevant maps are:

Landranger Luton, Hertford No. 166 scale 1: 50000

Pathfinder St. Albans No. 1119, and Harpenden No. 1095, are now replaced by one map. Explorer 182 to scale 1:25000

Definitive maps to scale 1: 10000 are available for inspection at Council Offices or libraries. Reference to these should be made whenever there is doubt about the route or status of any particular path.

GRID REFERENCES FOR CAR PARKS

Each of the 24 walks starts from a car park which is located by its Grid reference. To locate the car park, read the first three numbers of the reference along the top or bottom of the map in an easterly direction, i,e. from L to R. So 153 means from line 15, go three small divisions towards line 16. The last three numbers are read upwards using the lines on the L or R edges of the map, in a northerly direction. The intersection of these two directions gives the map location of the car park.

So G.R. 153,074 locates the Church. The bridge is on G.R. 158,075

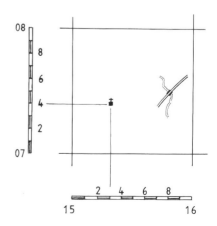

RIGHTS OF WAY ACT 1990

This act states that:

(a) Paths around the edge of a field must not be ploughed or disturbed.

(b) Paths across a field may be ploughed and cropped, but must be restored within 14 days.

(c) Restoration means making good the surface to make it usable by walkers. Moreover the line of the path must be apparent on the ground so that walkers can see where it goes through crops.

(d) The minimum path width must be 1 metre for a footpath across fields, and 1.5 metres for a footpath around a field edge.

If readers experience any problems concerning paths mentioned in this book, please notify the Footpaths Officer of the relevant Local Authority, and the Secretary of the Ramblers Association (see below). Quote the date, the Walks Booklet reference, and the location given by a six figure Grid Reference or a copy of the O.S. map, to highlight your problem.

Ramblers Association,
1/5 Wandsworth Road
London SW8 2XX
Tel: 020 7582 6878

REMEMBER THE COUNTRY CODE

Enjoy the countryside and respect its life and work.
Guard against all risk of fire.
Fasten all gates.
Keep your dogs under close control.
Keep to public paths across farmland.
Use gates and stiles to cross fences, hedges and walls.
Leave livestock, crops and machinery alone.
Take your litter home.
Help to keep all water clean.
Protect wildlife, plants and trees.
Take special care on country roads.
Make no unnecessary noise.

LEGEND

════	Motorway
═══	Main road
═══	Secondary road
= = = =	Track or Lane
▬▬ , ▬██	Railway
—□— —	O.H.P. Overhead power line
— — — — -	Path
══— - -	Fenced path
†	Church
✕	Signpost
∧	Waymark
⊢⊣	Stile
G	Gate
f. b.	Footbridge
P. H.	Public House
♀ ♀ ♀	Woodland trees
L , R	The walkers left or right when walking the specified route
N, S, E, W	Compass points
m	Metres
G , R	Grid Reference
C . P.	Car Park

CONTENTS

WALK 1

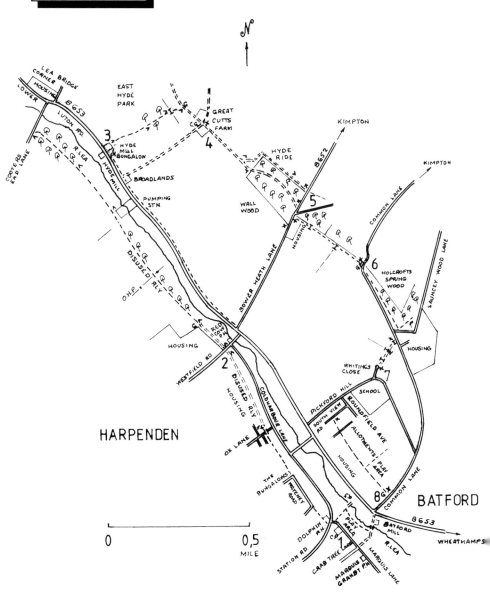

© Crown copyright

Total distance 4.5 miles (7.2km) or by the alternative route, 3 miles (4.8km)

HYDE MILL, BOWER HEATH AND BATFORD

WALK 1

Park at Marquis Lane car park, off Station Road, Harpenden.
G.R. 146,150

1 From the car park, cross Station Road, take the path (NW) on the W side of the Dolphin P.H. Pass Martham Court R along Hickling Way (NW). Continue straight ahead into Waveney Road, with grassy verge R, to junction with The Bungalows. Continue ahead on to the old railway track now part of the Upper Lea Valley Walk. This pleasant track crosses Ox Lane by a bridge and emerges eventually into Westfield Road. Note the Red Cow P.H. R.

2 Cross the road, and continue along the track (NW) then between hedges with views of the river R. Continue (NW) past the pumping station R, into woodland to Cooters End Lane at a waymark. Turn R along this lane (NE) cross the river, and at Lea Bridge Corner turn R (SE) along the Lower Luton Road B653 towards Wheathampstead. Keep to the R along this very busy road. In about 400m take the path L immediately opposite the gated entrance to Hyde Mill. Go round the bungalow then bear R uphill (NE) towards a small belt of trees.

3 Just beyond these cross the stile in a wire fence. Continue into a meadow (NE) to an asphalt access road. Turn R along this (SE) to a cattle grid and signpost at the crossing of tracks at Great Cutts Farm.

4 Continue ahead (SE) along the access road to the boundary of Wall Wood. Turn L, into a grassy ride and follow the boundary fence of the wood R (NE). At the corner of the wood, turn R (SE) and follow the fence R, This emerges on to Bower Heath Lane B652 at a signpost.

5 Turn R (SW) along the lane, then L just before a small grass island. Cross over and take the clear path in the woods at the side of a group of bungalows R (SE). At the edge of the woods cross a stile turn L and continue (SE) with woodland and hedge L. This emerges at a signpost by a stile in Common Lane.

6 Cross the lane turn R and in a few metres just before the road turns L, look for a squeeze gap in the wire fence L. (if this gap is closed continue down Common Lane to its junction with Sauncey Wood Lane). Go through, along a path through Holcrofts Spring Wood. (SE). This runs parallel with Common Lane R. Ignore a path which forks R, and continue ahead to emerge at a gap in the fence at the junction of Sauncey Wood Lane and Common Lane. Continue L along Common Lane (SE) and in a few metres cross to a signpost and stile R just before Sauncey Wood. Cross the stile, continue (SW) through a copse with fence L down to a stile, cross and go up to a signpost in Whitings Close.

7 Go down Whitings Close, turn R (SW) down Pickfords Hill passing a large school L. Take the second turning L, Roundfield Avenue (SE), then the first R South View Road (SW). In a few metres a clear path goes L between housing, passing allotments L, then a child's play area L (SE). It emerges on to Common Lane at a signpost.

8 Turn R along this lane to its junction with Wheathampstead Road B653. Turn L and in a few metres turn R in front of the Thatched Cottage. Continue (S) along the access road to Batford Mill. Cross the river by the footbridge (S) and immediately turn R along a clear path by the river (NW). Follow the river noting the weir R by the stepping stones. At the next footbridge do not cross but turn L along an asphalt path (SW). This leads to Marquis Lane opposite the car park.

Alternatively to shorten this walk, at item 2 turn R down Westfield Road, cross the Lower Luton Road, and go up Bower Heath Lane to item 5.

WALK 2

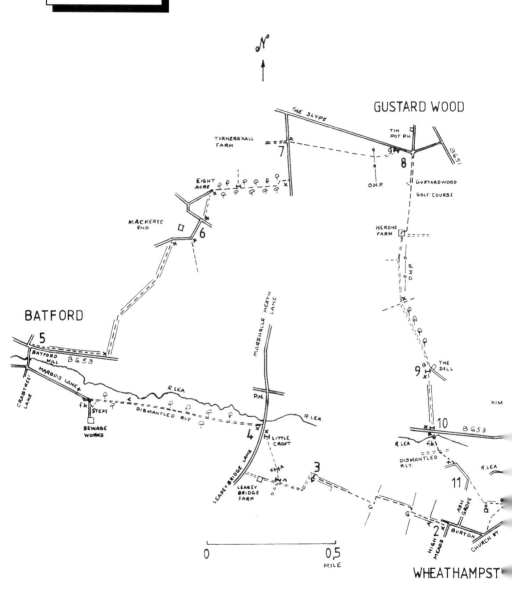

© Crown copyright

Total distance 6 miles (9.7km)

WHEATHAMPSTEAD, BATFORD AND MACKERYE END

Park in public car park in East Lane behind the Bull Inn
Wheathampstead. G.R. 128,141

1 From East Lane turn L up the High St (S). Go through the lych gate into the churchyard, and cross to the SW gate. Turn R into Church St, and in a few metres R again along Bury Green. Note the old school building now offices. Go past Ash Grove and take the next turning L High Meads. In a few metres take the path R marked by a signpost. This is part of the Upper Lea Valley Through Walk, notice the swan waymark.

2 The path (W) has a fence L and hedge R then crosses an open field. Go through the gate to a short R and L. Continue (W) with a tree lined hedge R. At the next transverse hedge turn L for a few metres to another gate. Go through and continue (W) along a grassy track over a field, then go between a wire fence L and hedge R.

3 At the next transverse track turn L at the swan waymark. This soon turns R and continues (W). This joins an access road leading to Leasey Bridge Farm. At the junction cross the stile R along a path (NW) across a small field, to another stile with yellow waymark. Cross this, continue (NW) to a third stile by a bungalow called Little Croft. This leads to Leasey Bridge Lane in which turn R to the bridge which offers a pleasant view of the river Lea.

4 Return to the old railway track which is the continuation of the Lea Valley Walk, and at the swan waymark continue (W) along the bridleway which gives further views of the river. The path continues by a bridge over the access road to a sewage works. Here turn L down steps go under the bridge into Marquis Lane (NW). At the Marquis of Granby P.H. turn R along Crabtree Lane (N) and cross the river by the footbridge. Notice the thatched cottage at the junction with the Wheathampstead road B653.

5 Cross this road and turn R (E) on to the footpath on the far side. In 300m a signpost shows a path on L (N). Take this path uphill between hedges. It emerges on to a road along which turn R. The road bears L past Mackerye End House with its fine gardens and variety of trees.

6 At the next T-junction turn R and in a few metres is a footpath L (N) which passes Holly Bush cottage. This meets an access road (N) which passes some very attractive houses. At its end is Eight Acre where a path goes R (E). This pleasant tree lined path emerges on to Marshalls Heath Lane along which turn L (N).

7 In about 300m opposite the entrance to Turners Hall Farm is a pleasant grassy path R (E) across a field. At the field corner, continue ahead past allotments L into a gravel track which meets a road called the Slype. Here turn R for Gustard Wood Common (E). Note the house called 'Hogs Island' L.

8 At the cross roads, divert L for the Tin Pot P.H. Retrace your steps to the cross roads, continue (S) along the access road to the cottages R, with golf course L. This continues (S) into a wide track leading to the access road to Herons Farm. Turn R into the farm, then L to a wide gravel track (S). This track continues (S) past a signpost to the iron gate at Dell Farm.

9 Do not go along the road, instead cross the stile just before the house called 'The Dell' and continue (S) across the field to a stile on the B653 road.

0 Cross the road to an asphalt footpath which crosses the river Lea by a footbridge. This continues (SE). At the road junction turn L.

1 When this road turns R, the footpath continues (SE) across a playing field, into the churchyard. Either way round this Parish Church of St Helens leads to the lych gate. Turn L down the High Street back to the car park.

WALK 3

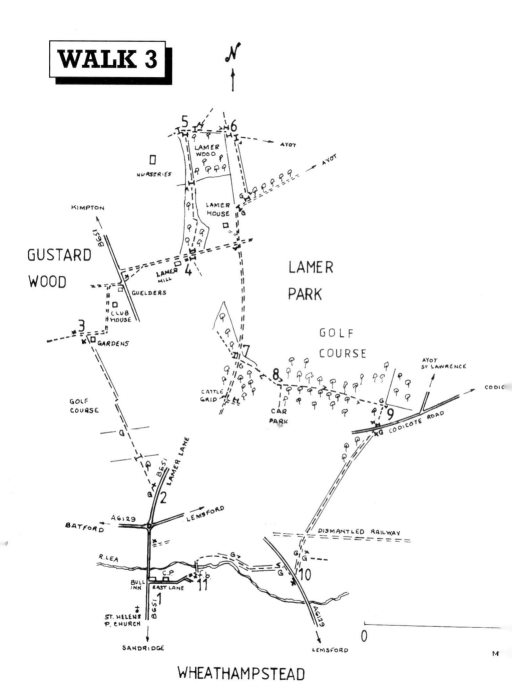

© Crown copyright

Total distance 4.7 miles (7.6km)

GUSTARD WOOD AND LAMER PARK

Park in public car park in East Lane behind the Bull Inn, Wheathampstead. G.R. 178,141

1 From East Lane, turn R along the High Street, cross the river Lea noting the old corn mill opposite. Continue along Lamer Lane (N). Opposite the large wrought iron gates to Lamer House is a kissing gate and signpost.

2 Take this path L and continue over a meadow (N). Cross the stile in the next crossing hedge, take the clear path ahead across a field (N) to a kissing gate. This leads to the golf course L with hedge R, then iron railings.

3 At the signposted transverse track, turn R (E) past the house called 'Gardens'. The track bears L (N) past the club house R. At the tee junction turn R, and at 'Guelders' with its post box, cross Lamer Lane to the signpost opposite. Continue past weather boarded cottages into an asphalt road (NE) in Lamer Park.

4 Pass 'Lamer Hill' and after a further 40m at the boundary of the wood R, turn L (N) over a stile to a footpath in the woods. Cross a stile in a transverse fence, continue (N) following a wire fence R.

5 At the boundary of the woods cross a stile. Ignore the stile L, instead turn R (E) following the edge of the wood. Cross the stile (E) ignoring a stile L. Continue between wire fences, and turn R to cross another stile at the corner of the wood, again ignoring a stile L.

6 Continue (S) with boundary of wood R. Follow the fence L to an iron gate and stile in L corner of the meadow. Note the fine avenue of trees on L. Turn R along this avenue and in a few metres meet an asphalt road where turn L (S). At the crossing of tracks on the corner of Lamer House, bear L along the wide gravel track (S) towards woodland.

7 Immediately on entering the woodland, turn L (E) through the gate in the wire fence, along a footpath on the inside edge of the wood. Continue (E) along a line of pines past the golf car park R.

8 Ignore the crossing track, continue ahead through woodland (E) alongside an avenue of beeches R. At the edge of the wood cross the golf course (E).

9 At the junction of two areas of woodland turn R through the gate in the high wire fence. Keep close to the fence R and continue (S) to the signpost at the Codicote Road. Cross the road to a wide gravel track (S) past newly planted trees and wire fence R. Continue across the dismantled railway, down to a gap by an iron gate. Go under the bridge carrying the Cory Wright Way.

0 Immediately after the bridge, turn R either up the steps, or by the nearby signpost, to the fenced bridleway which follows the road (NW). Turn L through the gate at the swan waymark, and continue (W) between wire fences with views of the river L. At the gap in the hedge, is a permissive path leading to the river bank. A clear path follows the river to a footbridge.

1 Cross the bridge on to an asphalt track (W) passing an outbuilding. Continue along Meads Lane, past Mead Hall and so to the car park.

WALK 4

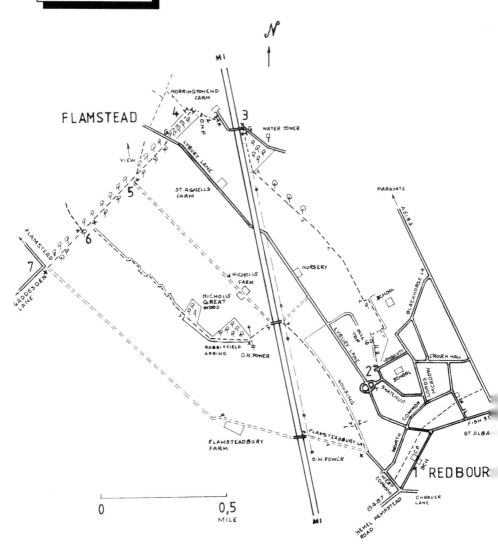

© Crown copyright

Total distance 4.75 miles (7.6km)

14

REDBOURN AND FLAMSTEAD

Park in car park on Redbourn Common near the cricket pavilion, opposite the old school. G.R. 103,119

WALK

4

1 From the pavilion take the asphalt path NE to the next crossing road Lybury Lane, along which turn L. Continue (NW) passing Brache Close and Down Edge to a circle of houses. Turn R into Terrace and Ridge Down by the telephone box, then L into Snatchup to its junction with Long Cutt. Cross to the path opposite by the signpost to Flamstead.

2 This path crosses a play area and goes into the Hilltop housing estate. At number 60 turn R on to a path (E) and in 100m turn L to follow the school's playing field fence R. This clear track goes across fields (NW) with a water tower ahead. Cross under the power lines and at the M1 boundary fence continue into a path between this fence and a plantation R. Continue (N) along the fence to a stile and signpost in a farm road.

3 Cross this stile and turn L along the road towards Norrington End Farm. Cross the bridge over the MI, and in about 150m, just before a cottage cross a stile L at a signpost. Cross a small field (SW) and at the cottage boundary turn R at waymark into a meadow (W). Look for a local power line post with a wood behind it and continue down to a corner of this wood (W).

4 Here cross a stile and follow a clear path (SW) inside the wood between wire fences. This emerges into Lybury Lane at a gate. Cross the lane and enter a green track opposite (SW) which can be muddy in wet weather. At the junction with another track note the fine view of Flamstead (N) through a gap in the hedge.

5 In a few metres (SW) at a junction, ignore the wide track which goes SE to Nicholls Farm, but continue along the track (SW) for about 400m to a signpost L.

6 Still on this same track (SW) continue to a road corner with a sign for Flamsteadbury.

7 Here turn L (SE) along the access road which crosses open fields to Flamsteadbury Farm, and leads to a bridge over the M1. Cross this into Flamsteadbury Lane on to West Common and the car park.

Alternatively A
At item 5 turn L along the wide track (SE) which goes through Nicholls Farm. Cross the M1 bridge, and at the power line take the path (SE) along the boundary fence of the housing into Flamsteadbury Lane, on to North Common and the car park.
Total distance 4 miles (6.41m).

Alternatively B
At item 6 turn L at signpost (SE) along a hedge L past the boundary of Nicholls Great Wood L. Soon where the wood boundary goes sharp R, look for a clear winding path (E) inside the edge of the wood. At the far corner by a local power line, emerge from the wood into a clear path which goes (NE) to the bridge over the M1. Cross this and at the power line take the path (SE) along the boundary fence of the housing into Flamsteadbury Lane, on to North Common and the car park.
Total distance 4.5 miles (7.2km).

15

WALK 5

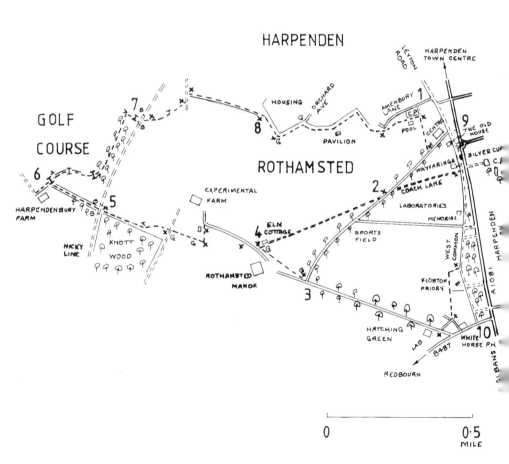

© Crown copyright

Total distance 3.5 miles (5.6km)

or by the alternative route via Hatching Green 4 miles (6.4km)

ROTHAMSTED AND HARPENDENBURY

Park in public car park in Amenbury Lane, Harpenden.
G.R. 133,141, or on Harpenden Common G.R. 137,138.

1 From the car park take the footpath (S) past the swimming pool into Rothamsted Park. Turn R along the fine avenue of trees (SW) to a crossing track marked by concrete posts. In a few metres take the fork R at the bridleway signpost. (If parked on the Common, cross the main St Albans Road (W) into Coach Lane alongside 'Wayfarings'. Continue (W) to item 2.

2 This wide track leads to Elm Cottage at a road junction item 4.
Alternatively you may prefer to continue along the avenue of trees (SW) to a road junction item 3.

3 At this junction turn R and in a few metres note a gate and sign R. Go through this gate, keep to the fence L, and continue to Elm Cottage at a signpost item 4.

4 A few metres (S) of the cottage is a transverse road, turn L along it if you wish to view Rothamsted Manor. Retrace your steps and continue along this road (NW) past the cottage R. In a further 0.5km the road turns sharp R, here turn L along a track (S). In about 110m turn R at a signpost. Continue (W) through two gates, cross a farm road and go towards a wood (W). The path now bears R and continues along the edge of Knott Wood (NW) to the 'Nicky Line' a disused railway track.

5 Cross this and go down a path between fences (NW). Where this track turns sharp L note a stile on R. If you miss this and continue to Harpendenbury Farm, retrace your steps when this stile is then more obvious.

6 Cross this stile, continue (NE) over pasture with fence L. At the edge of the wood is another stile L. Cross this and keep to a path (N) through this wood adjacent to the golf course. On emerging from the wood at a waymark sign, turn R towards the power line. Cross a stile and go along the edge of a field (E) and in a few metres cross the 'Nicky Line' again.
Alternatively a slightly shorter route is to go from item 5 along the Nicky Line direct to item 7.

7 Cross over and continue (E) along a wide well-marked track with fence R. This bends (NE) to a farm road in which turn L. In a few metres turn R along a hedge R.

8 At the end of the fields turn R at a signpost along a boundary hedge L bordering housing. Go through a gap in the hedge, turn sharp L then go through a gate into the park. Keep alongside a hedge L, go past the cricket pavilion, and the gate in Orchard Avenue. Continue with hedge L until reaching a second pavilion. Take the gravel track past the tennis courts L, and the sports field R. Finally go past the swimming pool R and return to the car park L.

9 **Alternatively** from the main entrance to Rothamsted Park, some interesting buildings are visible along Leyton Road (S) and West Common.

0 At the junction with Redbourn Lane B487 turn R, go past the White Horse P.H. and Hatching Green. Turn R into the access road leading to Rothamsted Manor to rejoin the walk at item 3.

WALK 6

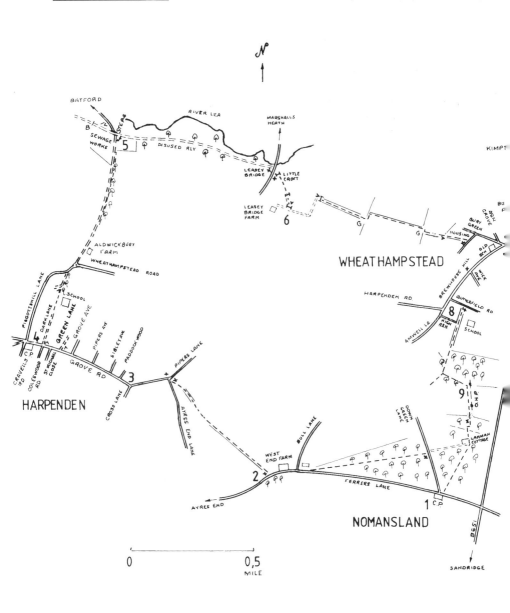

© Crown copyright

Total distance 6 miles (9.7km)

NOMANSLAND, HARPENDEN AND WHEATHAMPSTEAD

Park in public car park on Nomansland Common, at junction
of Down Green Lane and Ferrers Lane. G.R. 171,124

1 Go up Down Green Lane (N) for about 200m to a transverse bridleway. Turn L at the signpost (W) through woodland. Avoid forks and continue (W) into Ferrers Lane. Go past the junction with Bull Lane and West End Farm R.

2 After 150m past the farm, turn R along a wide track at a signpost (NW). This continues with hedge L into a road junction with Pipers Lane.

3 Continue (W) along Grove Road on a footpath R, passing Cross Lane L. The sixth turning R is Dark Lane.

4 Turn R along Dark Lane (N) passing a school R. This lane becomes an asphalt path through trees, and emerges on to Piggottshill Lane, here turn R to a small roundabout. Cross and continue past Aldwickbury Golf Course R, where the path narrows and goes downhill. Further on there is a pleasant path through trees parallel to the road.

5 At the sewage plant, note the old railway bridge ahead. Go up the steps on to the old railway track, turn R (E). This is part of the Upper Lea Valley Walk, and the track continues (E) to Leasey Bridge Lane at the swan waymark. At the lane divert to L to view the river from the bridge. Then retrace your steps (S) up the lane passing the Gatehouse L. At the bungalow called 'Little Croft' turn L at the signpost. Cross the stile and bear L across the field along a clear path (S). Cross another stile, then with hedge R a third stile into the farm access road. Note Leasey Bridge Farm R.

6 Turn L (E) along a wide track with a wire fence on each side. This track makes a short L and R round a field, then goes E at the waymarked post with hedge L and fence R. Go through a swing gate in the hedge, turn L and in a few metres R (E) following a hedge L. Continue through another gate to the boundary of the housing L and wooden fence R. The path meets a road at a signpost. Turn L and at the junction with Bury Green turn R, go downhill into Church Street.

7 Turn sharp R round the old school now converted to offices, go up Brewhouse Hill, take the second turning L which is Butterfield Road (E).

8 In about 200m note a signpost R at a path which goes S along the boundary of a former school L. This clear path continues into woodland, then turns L (E) along the edge of the wood, to a power line post.

9 At this post turn R along the edge of a field following the power line. The path enters woodland past a signpost. Continue (S) through the woods to Lanman Cottage. Ignore the track R, continue (SW) through the woods back to Ferrers Lane at the car park.

Note: alternative car parking is available starting from East Lane car park in Wheathampstead near item 7, or from Cravells Road car park at junction with Grove Road in Harpenden near item 4. The Upper Lea Valley Walk item 5 to 7 are included in walk number 2.

19

WALK 7

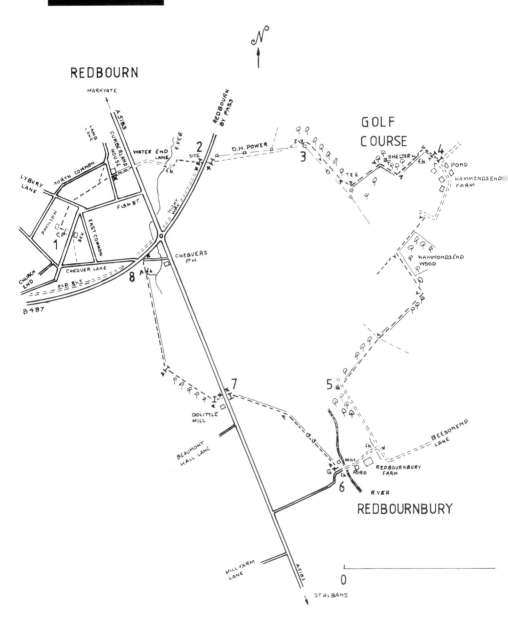

© Crown copyright

Total distance 4.5 miles (7.2km)

REDBOURN AND REDBOURNBURY

Park in public car park on Redbourn Common, near cricket pavilion opposite the old school. G.R. 103,119

1 From the pavilion take the clear asphalt path (NE) across the common. Cross Lybury Lane, and keep straight ahead to a transverse road. Continue past Cumberland House L along a path (E) between brick walls called The Ruins, to the High Street. Cross to Waterend Lane opposite. Go down this lane, cross the River Ver by the footbridge and in about 40m is a nursery. The path turns L then in a few metres R. Go past the gypsy site L to the old railway track called the Nicky Line, cross this at the stile and go on to the by-pass.

2 Cross the by-pass to the steps opposite, go over the stile to a field path. Continue (E) along the path under the power line to a hedge R. At the end of the hedge, continue towards the wood R.

3 At the point where the power line changes direction, turn L go through the hedge at the corner pole, by a white waymark sign. The path continues R (SE) through woods bordering the golf course. This emerges on to the edge of the course at a Tee and continues (E) with trees R behind a wooden shelter. Turn R past fruit trees, bear L then sharp R along a boundary fence R. Cross a stile in this fence opposite the large Hammondsend House. Cross a small meadow and stile (SE) into Hammondsend Lane.

4 Turn R go past Hammonds End House and farm R (S). The track turns R, and in a few metres L (SW) round the edge of a wood. At the corner of the wood turn L along its boundary (SE). At the bottom of the field turn R (SW) passing three trees in the hedge L. Continue with hedge R to a crossing access track.

5 Turn L along this track (SE) with trees R, towards the buildings in Redbournbury Farm. Turn R along the N side of the farm, and cross a footbridge. In about 90m cross two more bridges over the River Ver to Redbournbury Mill R.

6 Turn sharp R at the signpost go through the wooden gate (N) passing the mill R along a clear hedged track. Cross two gates, and the field path continues (N) with views of the river. This path bends NW and emerges on to the A5183 at a stile.

7 Cross the road to Dolittle Mill, turn R over a stile into a meadow, and follow a hedge L (NW). At the next stile continue (N) along a clear path with hedge R to the Redbourn by-pass. Note the Chequers P.H. R.

8 Cross this, turn L along Chequer Lane (W) passing the Nicky Line. Cross East Common and in a few metres turn R along a path crossing a children's play area to the old school. Opposite is the car park, the start of the walk.

WALK 8

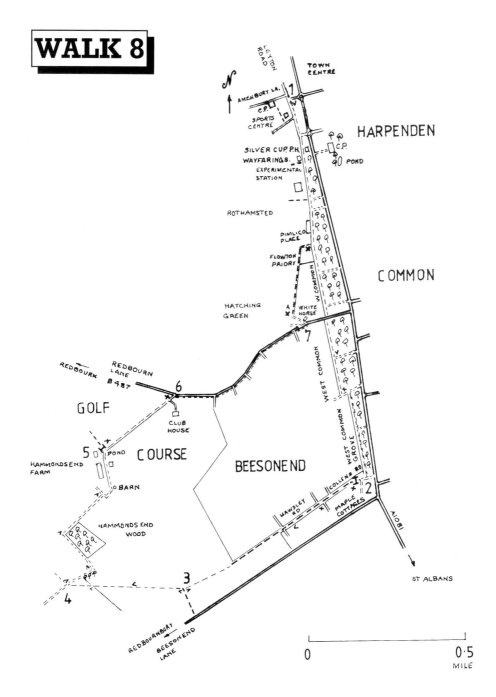

© Crown copyright

Total distance 4.9 miles (7.9km)

HARPENDEN AND
HAMMONDS END

Park in public car park in Amenbury Lane, Harpenden.
G.R. 133,141 or on Harpenden Common G.R. 137,138.

1 From the car park, take the footpath (S) into Rothamsted Park. Turn L along the avenue of trees, go past the Sports Hall L, and out through the main entrance into Leyton Road. Turn R along this road (S). Continue into West Common noting the Rothamsted Laboratory R. Continue past the attractive group of cottages called Pimlico Place R, and the extensive Flowton Priory. Cross Redbourn Lane and continue (S) along West Common. At the next road junction, a short L and R leads to West Common Grove. Notice the footpath parallel to this road just inside the tree line which you may prefer to use.

2 At the junction with a short access road leading to Maple Cottages, turn R and go past the end of the cottages L (SW). Cross the stile ahead, into the Beesonend Estate. Continue (SW) along Collens Road into Hawsley Road, ignore transverse roads and enter a track which runs (SW) along the rear of housing. This clear path continues across a field (SW) and is much used. A waymark sign marks the transverse path from Beesonend Lane.

3 Continue (W) along a clear track through a field, go through a gap in a transverse hedge at a waymark sign, and so downhill to a transverse track at another waymark.

4 Turn sharp R (NE) along this track with trees L. Continue with hedge R. The track turns sharp L along the boundary of Hammondsend Wood R. Turn R (NE) along the northern boundary of the Wood. At the next junction turn R, and in a few metres turn L passing a large barn R. Continue (N) past Hammonds End Farm and House L.

5 Turn R along the farm access road ignoring the stile L. This road passes the Golf Club House and leads to Redbourn Lane.

6 Turn R (E) along Redbourn Lane. There is a pleasant path on the R side of the road past some fine houses, leading to Hatching Green.

7 Here turn L along the lane (NW) at the White Horse P.H. R. At the end of the row of cottages, is the junction with the access road to Rothamsted Manor. Here turn R along a pleasant gravel footpath (N) at the signpost. This meets West Common alongside the row of cottages in Pimlico Place, and so back to the car park.

Note: Continuing (N) along Leyton Road leads to the shopping centre of Harpenden.

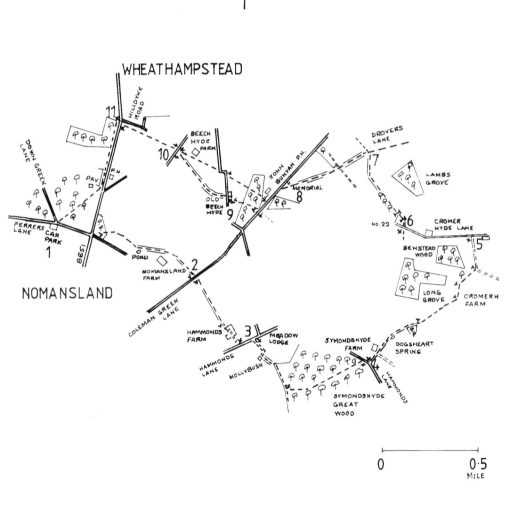

© Crown copyright

Total distance 6.5 miles (10.5km)

NOMANSLAND, SYMONDSHYDE AND COLEMAN GREEN

WALK 9

Park in car park on Nomansland Common, at junction of Down Green Lane, with Ferrers Lane. G.R. 171,124

1 Walk (E) along Ferrers Lane to the crossroads junction with B651. Take path (E) through small group of trees. This soon becomes a clear bridleway past Nomansland Farm into Coleman Green Lane.

2 Cross this lane and continue (SE) along a clear bridleway into a farm track leading to Hammonds Farm. Go through the gateway, follow the waymarking between farm buildings into the access road to Hammonds Lane. Turn L (NE) along this lane for about 100m.

3 Turn R (SE) into a gravel access road at Meadow Lodge, and pass May Cottage. At the entrance to Hollybush, turn L (E) along the boundary fence on a path which may be overgrown, into Symondshyde Great Wood. Turn R at Hollybush nameplate into a clear path along the boundary fence of this wood (S). Continue under a power line to a junction with a waymarked track. Here turn sharp L (E) along a wide track which goes (NE) into Hammonds Lane at a gate.

4 Turn R (SE) along this lane and after a few metres turn L (NE) along the access road to Symondshyde Farm. Continue (NE) passing the farm and derelict cottage L, into a meadow passing a small pond R called Dogsheart Spring. Continue (NE) with fence R passing a small wood R. At the far corner of the wood is a solitary tree L, here cross the field (NE), and continue N at the waymark, into the access road to Cromerhyde Farm. Turn L along this track (N) into Cromerhyde Lane.

5 Turn L along this lane (W) passing the cottages of Cromerhyde, to a signpost opposite No. 22.

6 Here turn R through the large gate into the gravel entrance, go past the house L to a stile just beyond a gate. Cross and continue diagonally across a small field to a second stile, then L to a cottage boundary fence. Turn R and continue (NW) along a raised bank L passing three large trees. Continue (N) with hedge L to a sunken lane called Drovers Lane.

7 Turn L along this lane (W) which crosses a transverse track and ends at the John Bunyan Chimney R.

8 At the junction with Coleman Green Lane, continue (SW) past the John Bunyan Public House R. Take the track (SW) parallel with the road passing Coleman Green Cottages R. In about 50m just beyond a telegraph post is a waymark post. Turn R along a path through the trees (W). Ignore tracks leading off, continue (W) into a field. Cross this to a waymark post. Bear L along a garden fence into a crossing lane by a signpost, alongside Old Beech Hyde.

9 Turn R along this lane, and in a few metres turn L into a wooded path (NW) opposite this house. This path opens into a headland path with hedge R and leads to a crossing lane alongside Beech Hyde Farm. Turn R in this lane and in a few metres turn L on to a field path opposite the gravel drive of this farm.

10 This clear path continues (NW) along a housing boundary fence R into Hilldyke Road at the junction with the Wheathampstead road B651.

11 Cross the road and take the well-marked path L (S) parallel to the road. This path continues (S) parallel with the road and emerges on to Nomansland Common opposite the Wicked Lady P.H. Here go (SW) through the Common to the car park at the junction of Ferrers and Down Green Lane.

Alternatively: at the John Bunyan P.H. item 8, take the path alongside Coleman Green Cottages (NW) through the woods. Continue (NW) straight across a field by a clear path into a lane at a bend. Go straight ahead along this lane. After about 40m at a sharp R bend, continue straight ahead along a clear track (NW) to Beech Hyde Farm into the poplar-lined access road of this farm. At the junction with the lane continue the walk from item 10, a slightly more direct route.

WALK 10

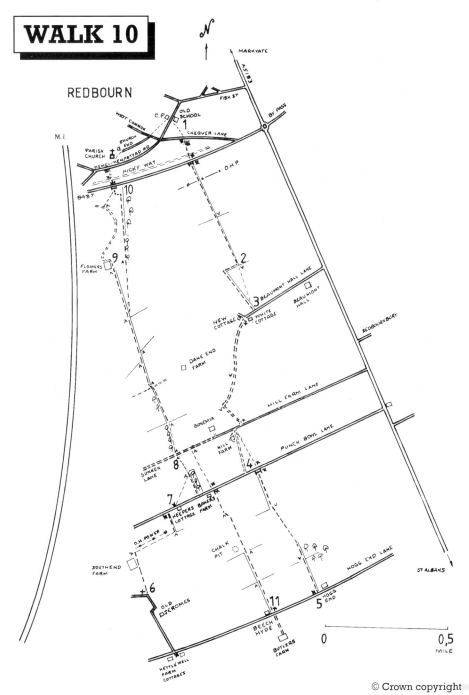

© Crown copyright

Total distance 5.5 miles (8.9km) or by the shorter alternative 5 miles (8.1km)

REDBOURN TO HOGG END LANE

Park in public car park on Redbourn Common near the cricket pavilion opposite the old school. G.R. 103,119

1 Starting from the old school building now offices, take the path (S) across the children's play area. Cross Chequer Lane, and, continue (S) through a swing gate between housing. Cross the gravel track which is part of the 'Nicky Line', and the embankment using the steps, Cross the bypass, go up the steps opposite to a stile with a signpost. Cross this and continue (S) to a field corner where there is a waymark. Continue (S) through a gap in the hedge, with hedge L to the corner of the next field.

2 Here the definitive path goes (S) across the next field to Beaumont Lane. If standing crops are impassable, you may prefer to turn R with hedge L for about 100m (SW). Then turn L through a gap in the hedge, continue with hedge L (S) to Beaumont Lane.

3 Turn R along this lane, go past White Cottage L, then bear L down a green lane passing New Cottage R. This lane winds (S) to Hill Farm Lane, along which turn R to Hill Farm. Turn L (S) into the farm access road, then go round the farm buildings passing the farmhouse L and rejoin the access road (S). This leads to Punch Bowl Lane.

4 Turn L along this lane for about 90m, then at the signpost turn R. Follow the hedge R (S) to its end, then turn slightly L (SE) and cross an open field heading for the Abbey Tower seen in the distance, and a group of trees. Go past these L and go along a field track with hedge L to Hogg End Lane, noting Hogg End Farm L.

5 Turn R (SW) along this lane, go past Butlers Farm L, on to Kettlewells Farm Cottages. Turn R along the lane signposted 'Old Jeromes' passing this house R.

6 Where the lane turns sharp L, continue ahead along a wide farm track (N) passing Southend Farm L. At the farm boundary, turn R across a field (NE) following the power line L. At the hedge turn L (NW) to Punch Bowl Lane.

7 Turn R along the lane for about 50m to a signpost L just before Keepers Cottage. Enter the field and cross diagonally (NE) to the corner of a small wood. This is a definitive path, if however you find growing crops impassable, you may prefer to continue along the lane for about 100m, then turn L in front of this wood to the same corner. Here look downhill (NW) for a waymark in a hedge. Walk to it into a sunken lane.

8 Cross this lane to the waymark opposite and follow the line of trees ahead (N). When Dane End Farm is in a NE direction at a field corner, turn L through a gap in the hedge. Continue (N) with the hedge R towards Flowers Farm.

9 Continue along the farm access road (N). When this road curves (W) bear R (NE) across the corner of a field to a stile. Cross this and the stile opposite, go down the steps and cross the by-pass. Go up the steps opposite over the embankment.

0 Cross the 'Nicky Line' gravel path, go along a short lane (N) to the Hemel Hempstead Road, and to Redbourn Parish Church. Cross into the churchyard (NE) to the gateway in Church End, noting the old cottages and Hollybush P.H. Continue (E), cross West Common Road and so to the car park ahead.

1 **Alternatively** a slightly shorter walk can be devised at item 5. In Hogg End Lane turn R (N) opposite Butlers Farm alongside Beech Hyde. This track goes (N) with hedge L across two fields to an old chalk pit L. Ahead is a white washed house called Bakers Farm. The path goes across an open field (N) passing this house L to a pipe gateway and signpost in Punch Bowl Lane. Cross to the signpost opposite, continue (NW) to the sunken lane then turn L to the waymarks item 8.

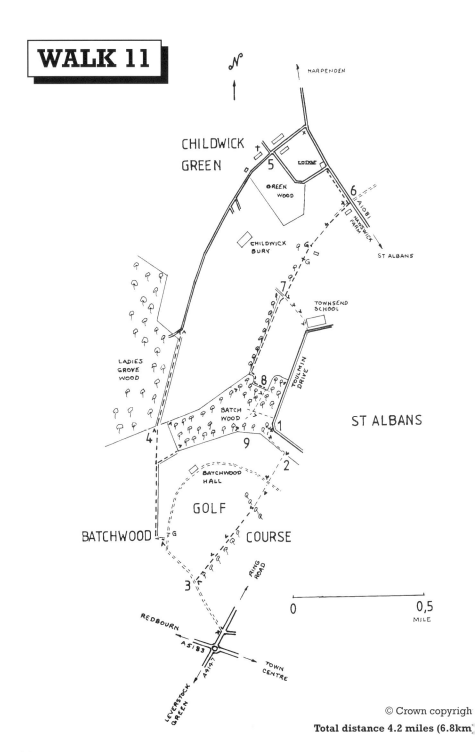

WALK 11

N

HARPENDEN

CHILDWICK GREEN

5

LODGE

GREEN WOOD

6

A1081

HAWSWICK FARM

ST ALBANS

CHILDWICK BURY

7

TOWNSEND SCHOOL

LADIES GROVE WOOD

8

TOULMIN DRIVE

BATCH WOOD

ST ALBANS

4

9

1

BATCHWOOD HALL

2

GOLF

BATCHWOOD

COURSE

RING ROAD

3

REDBOURN

A5183

TOWN CENTRE

LEVERSTOCK GREEN

A4147

0   0,5
              MILE

© Crown copyrigh

Total distance 4.2 miles (6.8km)

28

BATCHWOOD AND CHILDWICK GREEN

Park discreetly in Toulmin Drive, St. Albans adjacent to
Batch Wood. G.R. 141,092

1 Walk (S) down Toulmin Drive with Batch Wood (R), and where the road turns sharp L at number 18, continue (S) along a footpath with hedge and trees R. At a crossing chain link fence, turn L, keeping this fence R.

2 At a wide gap in this fence, turn R, and continue (SW) across the golf course. The route is liberally marked with waymark signs. Cross the Batchwood Hall access road, go through a narrow belt of trees and continue (SW) with belt of trees L to the access road by the signpost.

3 Turn R along this road and in 250m turn L at a signposted bridleway. This soon turns R along a footpath (N) with a hedge R along the boundary of the golf course. Ignore the path R, and continue along this well used path across a field to the corner of Ladies Grove Wood.

4 Continue (N) along a fenced path alongside the edge of the wood, into the access road which passes the large house Childwickbury, and leads to the hamlet of Childwick Green.

5 Near the pump turn R (SE) along a road lined with rhododendron bushes. The road bends L and meets the St. Albans to Harpenden road by Childwick Lodge. Turn R and walk along the footpath/cycle path (SE) alongside the road for about 300m to Hawswick Farm.

6 Turn R at the farm entrance along the gravel track (SW) to the boundary fence, to a wooden gate in the corner of the field. Turn L through the gate along the farm boundary fence into a wide track between hedges (SW). Go through the large iron gate and continue (SW) to emerge from a narrow belt of trees.

7 Here a bridleway leads (SE) to school playing fields into Toulmin Drive down which you reach the start of the walk.

Alternatively a more interesting route is to continue (SW) alongside a belt of trees R with an open field L. Follow the boundary of the trees to a corner where the tree line runs N.

8 At this corner a small path runs (SW) into the wood for about 200m to a crossing path by a large oak with a waymark. Here turn L for a further 200m through the wood to the start in Toulmin Drive.

9 **Note:** There is now a permissive path around Batch Wood indicated by posts with white arrows.

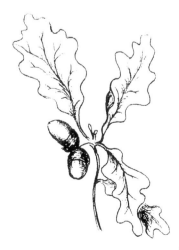

WALK 12

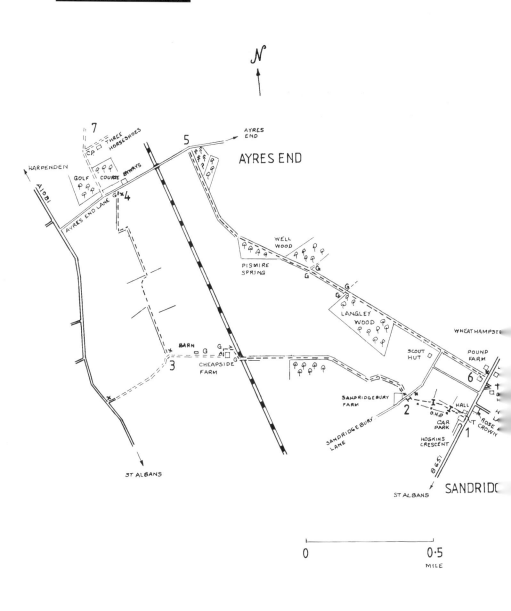

© Crown copyright

Total distance 4.3 miles (6.8km)

Starting from the Three Horseshoes 4.5 miles (7.2km)

WEST OF SANDRIDGE

Park in public car park in Sandridge by the village Hall, where there are toilets and a public telephone. G.R. 169,104

1 From the car park go along the fence of the recreation ground (W) with hedge R. Cross two stiles and follow the power line (W) to a third signposted stile in Sandridgebury Lane.

2 Immediately opposite at another signpost, the path continues (W) between fences or hedges past a small plantation L. A short length with hedges on both sides leads to a brick bridge over the railway. Cross this and go through the wooden gate. Look for a farm gate ahead (NW) alongside a group of farm buildings L. Go through this gate L and the farmyard, and on to the access road of Cheapside Farm. Turn R along this road (W) and go through another gate. In about 400m where the road turns L there is a track R.

3 Turn R and go along this track (N) with hedge L. Cross an open field to a hedge at the bottom. Turn R with hedge L for a few metres, then turn L through a gap in this hedge. Continue (N) with hedge L, into Ayres End Lane by a gate.

4 Turn R along this road, passing a house called 'Byways', and go over the railway bridge. In a further 300m, the road bears R and a track goes sharp R by a large felled tree trunk at a signpost.

5 This track continues (S) then (SE) past small areas of woodland. Ignore a transverse track at Langley Wood, and continue (SE) past the Scout Hut R. This leads to Sandridge Road at Pound Farm.

6 Here turn R, noting the Queen's Head P.H. L. The Parish Church of St. Leonard is worth a visit. Continue SW along St. Albans Road to the car park nearby. There are a number of Public Houses in Sandridge where refreshment is available.

7 **Alternatively** it is possible to park near the Three Horseshoes P.H. on Harpenden Golf Course G.R. 143,120. Then from item 4 one may continue via Sandridge returning from items 3 and 4 to the car park.

WALK 13

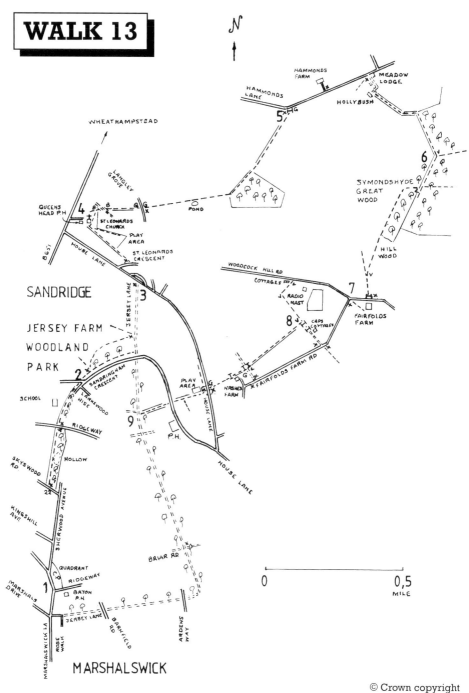

© Crown copyright

Total distance 6.5 miles (10.5km)

MARSHALSWICK, SANDRIDGE AND SYMONDSHYDE

Park in public car park at the Quadrant, Marshalswick, St. Albans. G.R. 169,086. Public toilets are available near the Library in The Ridgeway.

1 Go past the shops R along Sherwood Avenue (N) and pass Kingshill Avenue. At the next turning, Skyswood Road, turn L and in a few metres alongside number 41, turn R along a footpath through a small wood (N). Keep to the fence L and pass a small hollow R, and cross the transverse road The Ridgeway. Continue (N) along a wooded path by the boundary fence of School L.

2 This path emerges on to a road junction. Cross the road, turn R along Sandringham Crescent. After a few metres take the signposted path (NE) parallel with the road. In about 400m is a transverse asphalt track called Jersey Lane along which turn L (N). Ignore transverse footpaths and continue to its junction with House Lane.

3 Turn L along this lane, and take the next turning R called St. Leonards Crescent (NE). A few metres along this is a footpath L at a signpost. This goes along a boundary fence, past a small play area then a cemetery to the Parish Church of St. Leonard which is worth a visit.

4 Take the path R (N) along the E end of the church to the NE corner of the churchyard. Cross the transverse asphalt lane at the pipe rail barriers, and turn R (E) along a track with garages L and a hedge R. Cross Langley Grove into a wide grassy track opposite (E). Continue across open fields, past a small pond R, then enter a small wood. Continue (NE) with the boundary of the wood L. On emerging from the wood, the path continues with a ditch and hedge L.

5 Cross the stile into Hammonds Lane, turn R go past Hammonds Farm L. After a further 150m turn R (SE) into a gravel track at Meadow Lodge. Continue to the house called Hollybush then turn L (E) along the boundary fence between hedges on a path into Symondshyde Great Wood. Turn R at the corner of the wood (S) into a clear path inside the boundary fence of the wood R (S).

6 At the waymark post, ignore the track L and continue (S) along a broad track through the woods. In about 200m at a crossing track, turn R at the waymark. In a further 50m turn L (SW) inside the edge of the wood. This emerges on to a grassy track (S) leading to Fairfolds Farm. Cross the stile and turn R (W) along the road.

7 At the fork in the road turn L (S) passing the radio mast and buildings R. Soon a private road, which is a public right of way, turns R (NW) leading to Caps Cottages R. Cross two stiles ahead with boundary fence R, and immediately turn L after the second stile.

Alternatively at the fork in the road turn R and continue (E) along Woodcock Hill Road passing the radio mast L. At Fairfolds Farm Cottages turn L at the waymark sign, then L again round the boundary fence to the same stile where you turn R (SW) without crossing the stile.

8 Continue downhill SW with barbed wire fence L to a stile in a transverse track with stile opposite. Cross this into the field passing Nashes Farm L (SW) to another stile with fence L. Continue downhill bear L, cross the next stile and cross House Lane with care. Cross the stile opposite and a transverse gravel track, continue past a childs play area R. The path continues SW and soon becomes asphalt surfaced between housing. Cross the next road, and soon meet a pleasant transverse wooded track. This is Jersey Lane along which turn L (S).

9 This lane continues S between housing, crosses a bridleway and eventually turns R crossing Ardens Way and Barnfield Road. Just before crossing Rose Walk the lane becomes an asphalt surfaced access road. Continue ahead to meet Marshalswick Lane at the junction with Marshals Drive. Turn R (N) along this lane, cross the Ridgeway and so return to the Quadrant car park.

Here the shops are worth attention, and refreshments are available at the garage.

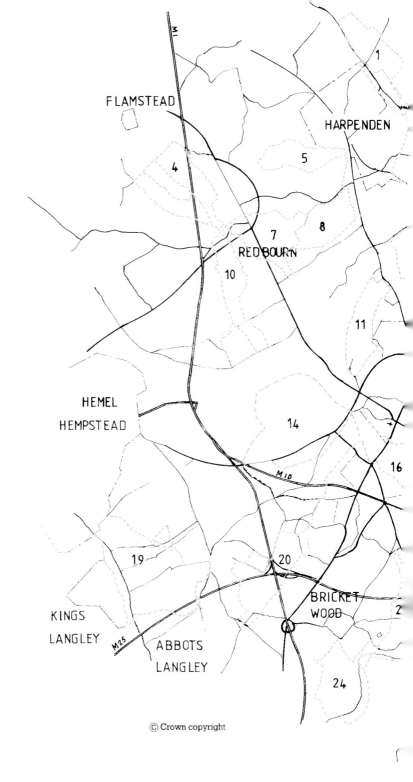

FLAMSTEAD

HARPENDEN

REDBOURN

HEMEL
HEMPSTEAD

KINGS
LANGLEY

ABBOTS
LANGLEY

BRICKET
WOOD

© Crown copyright

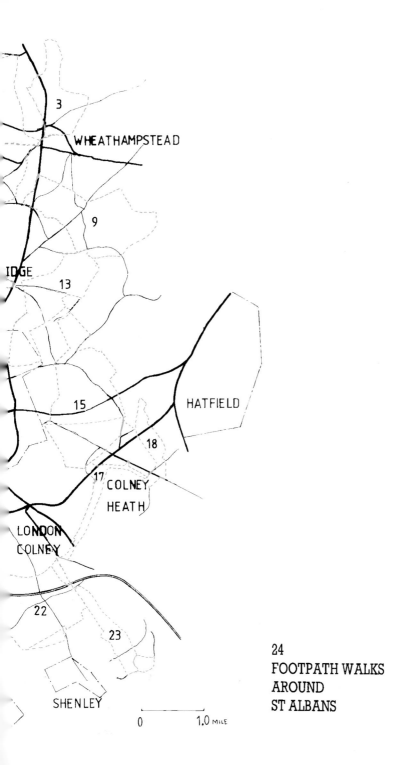

3

WHEATHAMPSTEAD

9

IDGE

13

15

HATFIELD

18

17 COLNEY
HEATH

LONDON
COLNEY

22

23

SHENLEY

0   1.0 MILE

24
FOOTPATH WALKS
AROUND
ST ALBANS

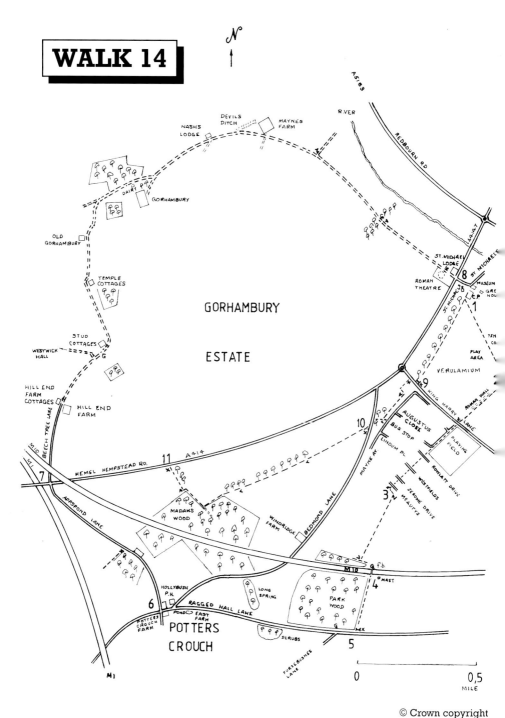

WALK 14

© Crown copyright

Total distance 6.5 miles (11km), or by a shorter route 5.5 miles (8.8km)

ST. MICHAELS, POTTERS CROUCH AND GORHAMBURY

WALK 14

Park in public car park new Verulamium Museum in St. Michaels village St. Albans. G.R. 136,073

1 Note Grebe House at the entrance to Verulamium. From the car park take the asphalt footpath (SE) with hedge L, past the tennis courts L, and a childrens play area R. Just beyond a signpost is a wide transverse asphalt track.

2 Turn R along this (SW) noting the outline of the Roman East Gate and wall ruins R. This track emerges on to the busy King Harry Lane which is crossed at the traffic lights. The path continues (SW) opposite, past the housing R, and a playing field L. Continue through housing across Rowlatt Drive, Westfields, Jerome Drive, and Meautys on to a grassy area.

3 Then after a short L and R, the clear path continues (SW) uphill over farmland towards a group of trees. At the edge of this wood a short L and R leads to a kissing gate and footbridge over the M10.

4 The path ahead (S) follows the boundary of Park Wood R and emerges at a signpost on to Ragged Hall Lane.

5 Turn R (W) along this pleasant lane, passing East Farm L. At the junction with Bedmond Lane is the Hollybush P.H.

6 Continue (W) along Bedmond Lane and in a few metres, at Potters Crouch Farm L, turn R noting the old cottages along Appspond Lane (N). This leads to the main cross road A4147 to Hemel Hempstead.

7 Cross the road with care into Beech Tree Lane opposite which leads (N) into the Gorhambury Estate. This road goes under the M10, past Hill End Farm R, and some fine half timbered cottages L. Continue (NW) past Stud Cottages L, Temple Cottages R, then past the ruins of Old Gorhambury L. Next along the road is the Old Dairy R, and Gorhambury House R. The road bears E past Nashs Lodge L, and the ancient Devils Ditch L alongside Maynes Farm. Ignore the next track L leading to the Ver Valley, continue along the road (SE) over the pleasant farming land. At the next belt of trees is a waymark. Eventually at the entrance gate is St. Michaels Lodge L, and the remains of a Roman Theatre R.

8 Cross the Hemel Hempstead Road at the traffic lights, into St. Michaels Street opposite. The next Turning R at the Museum leads to the car park.

Alternatively for a shorter route starting from the car park item 1, walk (SW) along the tree lined hedge R. Cross the stile in the crossing hedge into King Harry Lane.

9 Cross this road, turn R and in a few metres turn L (SW) at the housing boundary. Turn L again at the far end of the housing then R (SW) on a path parallel with Mayne Avenue. Go past Antonine Gate, and Claudian Place L to a bus stop near Augustus Close. Opposite is a path which turns off R (W) past a hollow in the trees, which meets Bedmond Lane. Turn L along this lane and in a few metres is a signpost R.

0 From here a clear path runs (SW) across two open fields. Head for a line of trees, note a waymark on the first tree. Follow this line of trees, and continue by a tree lined hedge L at another waymark. Follow the boundary of the wood L (SW) to a corner where the boundary turns R (NW). At the next corner of the wood, a short L and R leads to a path which goes NW. Again a line of trees R shows the route to a signpost on the Hemel Hempstead Road.

1 Turn L along this busy road, go under the M10 bridge, and immediately note a cross road. Here turn R into Beech Tree Lane item 7. Then continue through the Gorhambury Estate as above.

Note: This road through Gorhambury Estate is private. Lord Verulam permits walkers to use it, but reserves the right to close it on Saturdays from September to January. Check that access is possible from the notice board at St. Michaels Lodge item 8, before starting the walk.

WALK 15

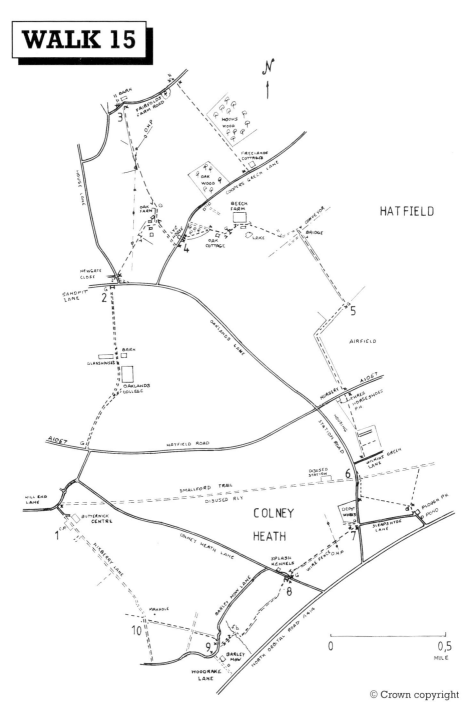

© Crown copyright

Total distance 7.3 miles (11.8km), or by the alternative Smallford Trail 6.2 miles (10km)

OAKLANDS, SMALLFORD AND SLEAPSHYDE

Park discreetly in Hixberry Lane near junction with Hill End Lane. G.R. 179,069

1 Return past the Butterwick Day Centre R, turn R into Hill End Lane (N). then L along Colney Heath Lane. Turn L into Hatfield Road, and cross to the main entrance gate of Oaklands College. Continue (N) along this pleasant drive, ignore a R fork, go past the College R. The drive continues as a wide gravel track (N) and meets Sandpit Lane at a stile with a gate.

2 Cross the road into the asphalt path opposite (NE) and in a few metres is the junction of Newgate Close with House Lane. Cross the lane to a signpost opposite this junction. Go through the gap in the hedge, and continue (NE) across a field. Go uphill (NE) past a power line post L, cross a stile towards Oak Farm. Go between two large barns ahead, past the farmhouse L to the access road. Turn L (N) along a clear track and pass the farm L. Continue (N) crossing under the power line. Note the large barn ahead and with wire fence L, meet Fairfolds Farm Road.

3 Turn R along the road (NE) to a signpost R opposite a private road entrance. Turn R (SE) across a field on a clear path noting a large wood ahead. The path meets the boundary of Hooks Wood L. At the far corner of this wood, continue across a field passing Freelands Cottages L, to a stile and signpost in the hedge bordering Coopers Green Lane. Turn R along this lane (SW) passing Oak Wood R. Pass the entrances to Beech Farm Drive and the gravel works L, and after a few metres in a small copse, is a stile L.

4 Cross this stile, and go through this copse (NE) to a transverse access road. Turn R (E) pass Oak Cottage R, and go through a gate and stile at the entrance to Beech Farm. Go past the farm L and continue (E) with quarry infill lake R. The track becomes a wide access road (NE) which crosses a conveyor belt at a small bridge. Go straight ahead along a wide path (SE) to the airfield boundary fence.

5 Turn sharp R at the gate and signpost (SW) continue with hedge and fence L. Turn L between chain link fences (SE) into Hatfield Road at the Nursery. Cross the road to a signpost and stile opposite noting the Three Horseshoes P.H., and continue (SE) with housing R. This clear path emerges on to Wilkins Green Lane where turn R to Station Road.

6 Turn L (S) along an asphalt path which slopes down to cross the old railway track. Continue (S) along a path with hedge R parallel with the road. At the next signpost turn L along a firm asphalt track (E) across a field. At the junction of paths turn R to the Plough P.H. in the hamlet of Sleapshyde. Turn R along Sleapshyde Lane (W). At the junction with Station Road cross to the stile with signpost.

7 Cross this stile to a clear path over Colney Heath (SW). Follow a wire fence L, cross under the power line and aim for a chalet bungalow ahead. Just to the L is a large metal stile and signpost. Cross this, go past an iron gate R into Colney Heath Lane.

8 Immediately opposite is a signpost and stile. Cross and go (SW) across a field to a hedge. Go round the hedge, and continue with hedge R (SW). The path eventually meets a small hidden stream, along which turn R to a small footbridge in a hedge. Turn L cross the bridge and continue (SW) between fences and over stiles into the lane.

9 Turn R along Barley Mow Lane (N) and in about 40m turn L (W) at a signpost just before the lane turns R. A clear path follows a hedge and ditch R (W). At a wide transverse track, turn R and immediately L along a path with hedge and ditch L (W). This leads to a transverse lane at concrete posts. Note the concrete manhole nearby. This is Hixberry Lane.

0 Turn R along this lane to the car park.

Alternatively at item 6 go down to the old railway line called the Smallford Trail, turn R (W) along this pleasant track to Hill End Lane. Turn L to the car park.

WALK 16

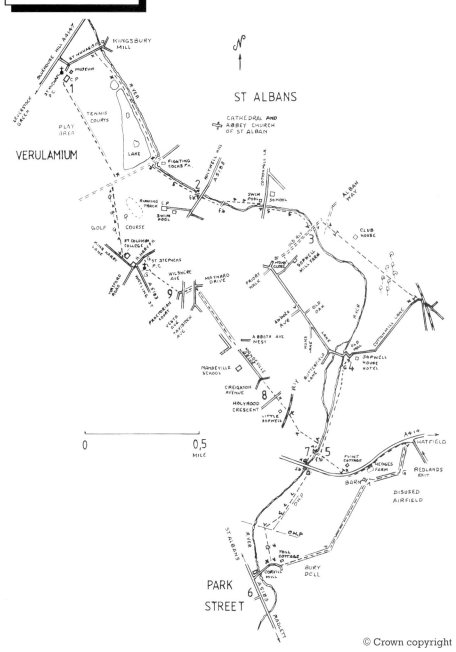

© Crown copyright

Total distance 7 miles (11.3km), or by the shorter route 5 miles (8km)

VERULAMIUM, RIVER VER AND PARK STREET

Park in public car park near the Verulamium Museum, St. Michaels. G.R. 136,073.

1 From the car park go N between the Museum and St. Michaels Church, turn R into St. Michaels Street. This area is called St. Michaels village and contains some interesting buildings. Opposite Kingsbury Mill, in the iron railings R is a gate leading into Verulamium Park (SE). Take this asphalt path between the lake and the river. At the SE corner of the lake, where a transverse track goes L to the Fighting Cocks P.H. and also to the Cathedral and Abbey Church, bear R (S) for a few metres. Go down the steps at the rear of the Public Toilets to the S bank of the river. This pleasant path continues SE to a footbridge at the bottom of Holywell Hill.

2 Cross the road with care, go through the gap in the wall opposite, and continue along the S bank of the river with a boundary fence R. Cross the steel footbridge to the N bank, and continue into Cottonmill Lane by the Council Swimming Pool. Cross the road, turn R, cross the river, turn L (E) down steps along the S bank of the river. On the R note the ruins on the site of Sopwell Nunnery. This path ends at the old railway arch, where steps lead up to the dismantled railway track.

3 Go up these steps and turn L along the track. At the boundary of the new housing estate, turn R down steps. Bear L on to a fenced path (SE), and cross the golf course. Go past the club house L, and continue (SE) with hedge R through a belt of trees into Cottonmill Lane. Turn R along this busy road (SW) passing Sopwell House Hotel, and Home Farm. At the bend in the road take the signed footpath L (S) the Ver/Colne path. **Alternatively** turn R along the old railway track (SW), and in about 300m steps lead down to a track L at the rear of housing. Turn R at the last house into Cottonmill Lane. Turn L (SE) and continue to the old mill buildings now an industrial estate. At the second bend in the road a signpost R leads to the Ver/Colne Walk as above.

4 Continue along the bank of the river R through a gate (S) to a footbridge.

5 Cross the bridge turn L (SW) through a gate under the A414. turn L over another bridge, turn R and follow the river bank R to a waymark. Bear L (SW) to another waymark near an electricity pole. Continue to follow waymarks with hedge L. Go through a gate passing allotments R to Toll Cottage. Turn R along the access road to Park Mill on the A5183 at Park Street. Here are public houses, shops and toilet facilities at the tee junction.

6 Retrace your steps past the mill L and at Toll Cottage go straight ahead (NE) up hill between wire fences. (Note the old Handley Page airfield R, now gravel workings). Bear L between hedge and fence to Hedges Farm giving good views of St. Albans. Continue between wire fences R then L to a gate on A414. Turn L along this busy road to Hedges Farm entrance. Turn R cross this road with care to Flint Cottages opposite. Cross the stile L and head for the footbridge, keeping to the headland if the ground is wet.

7 Cross the bridge turn R and in about 150m turn L at the waymark (NW). At the corner of a small wood by the railway embankment, follow the waymark R then L under a railway bridge at a signpost. Go past Little Sopwell L, along a row of trees R (NW) to a transverse road Holyrood Crescent.

8 Cross the road, go through the rear of housing across Creighton Avenue. Continue along Mandeville Drive, through rear of housing to Maynard Drive, where turn L to Tavistock Avenue. Cross this road and take the asphalt path (W) through housing to Vesta Avenue.

9 Cross this into Praetorian Court, and where this turns L bear R (NW) cross a ditch, and go over a field towards St. Stephens Church. Head for the very old cedar tree, and continue to the gate in the churchyard. Go through the churchyard and the main gate into Watling Street. Turn R and cross to the King Harry P.H. opposite. Go past this, turn R into King Harry Lane. At the far boundary of St. Columba's College bear R (N) on the waymarked path across the golf course in Verulamium Park. Continue N with trees L, then a hedge L, to a transverse asphalt track. Turn R, and in a few metres turn L (NW) past a child's play area to the Museum and the car park.
Note: to shorten this walk, cross the footbridge at item 5 and rejoin the walk at item 7, omitting the visit to Park Street.

WALK 17

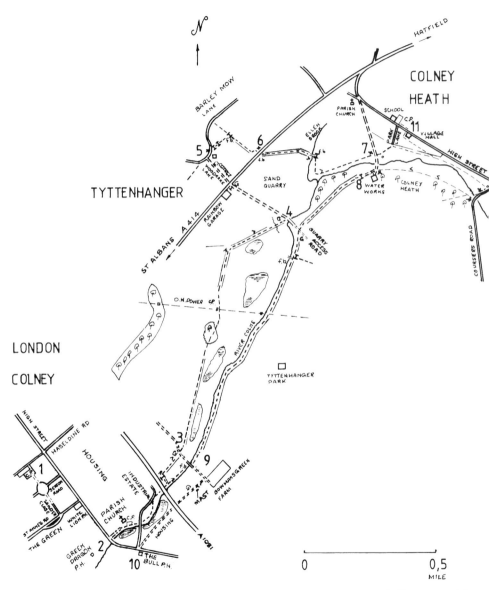

© Crown copyright

Total distance 6.5 miles (10.5km) or by the alternative route, 5.5 miles (8.9km)

Using the car park by St Peters Church, 5.6 miles (9km)

LONDON COLNEY, RIVER COLNE AND COLNEY HEATH

WALK 17

Park in public car park in Haseldine Road, London Colney. G.R. 177,041 or in car park by St. Peters Church G.R. 182,032 at item 2.

1 Take the asphalt path between housing at rear of car park (SE) go through the circle of housing to the path opposite (SE) which leads into Sanders Close. Where this meets The Green, turn L along St. Annes Road (NE). At the White Lion P.H. turn R into the High Street, and continue (SE) towards the river. Just before reaching the bridge, turn L past the Parish Church L.

2 A gravel track now follows the river bank (NE). Cross the access road leading to the industrial estate. The track meets another access road in a few metres, then continues (NE) along the river bank under the A1081 road bridge. At the far side continue (NE) along the river bank to the farm access road.

3 Turn L and in a few metres turn R (N) along a track with hedge or fence R. Head for the power line pylon, noting the lakes in the old quarry infill R. Continue (N) and where the track turns L, bear R into a new plantation. Go round the woodland past the pylon L. This path meets an access road where bear R (NE). Go past the drainage pond R to an iron gate L opposite Tyttenhanger Quarry.

4 Go through this gate, turn L and go along the concrete access (NW) with care. This is a right of way, and at the end of the road is a stile by an iron gate leading to the A414 by the Rainbow Garage. Cross the road into a narrow asphalt lane opposite, marked by iron posts. Continue (NW) past Woodrake Cottage into Barley Mow Lane.

5 At this junction turn R (NE) at the signpost into a path between fences. Cross the stiles to a small footbridge into a field, immediately turn R (SE). Cross a small ditch and continue (SE) with hedge and stream R. This bends L then almost immediately turn R through trees to a signpost on the A414. Cross the road to a small footbridge opposite.

6 Cross this bridge and continue ahead (E) on a fenced path between lakes. This leads to a footbridge over the Ellen Brook. Cross the bridge and stile, turn R (S) continue with river R and open field L. The path bears L (NE) along the bank of the river Colne into Church Lane. Cross over on to Colney Heath near coal post.

7 Continue (E) across the Heath with housing L and the river R to another coal post near the Cock P.H. Turn R and cross the river by the bridge in Coursers Road. Turn R again at the signpost and go (W) across the Heath with river R and woodland L. This pleasant path follows the river to the Water Works access road. Turn L along this road, go past the Water Works L and a group of houses R (SW).

8 Continue along a track with Works L, then after about 100m cross a stile into a field path with hedge R (SW). In about 0.5km is a large steel bridge R used by quarry vehicles. Cross the quarry access road and the conveyor belt. Bear L (S) go through the kissing gate near the bridge. Continue (S) with river R and wire fence L, heading for the power pylon. The path follows the river bank for about 2km passing Tyttenhanger Park L.

9 The path leads to Bowmansgreen Farm L. Continue to the farm concrete access road. Turn L towards the farm (SE) and turn R to the radio mast. Go past this L (SW) to another access road which continues under the A1081 road bridge. Continue (SW) along a road with housing L, lakes and river R, to the High Street opposite the Bull P.H.

0 Turn R along the High Street, cross the river by the so-called Telfords Bridge. Note the picturesque Waterside L. Continue past the White Lion P.H. (NW) and return to Haseldine Road. Turn L for the car park.

1 **Alternatively:** This walk can be started from Colney Heath. Park in public car park next to Colney Heath School G.R. 201,061. From here cross the road, turn L along the High Street to the village hall. Turn R then L along the Heath with river R. Cross the road at Coursers Road bridge and continue to items 8, 9, 10. At item 10 cross the bridge to item 2 if you do not wish to visit London Colney. Continue then to item 7. At the coal post go (E) across the Heath for about 50m into Park Lane. This leads to the High Street opposite the car park.

WALK 18

N

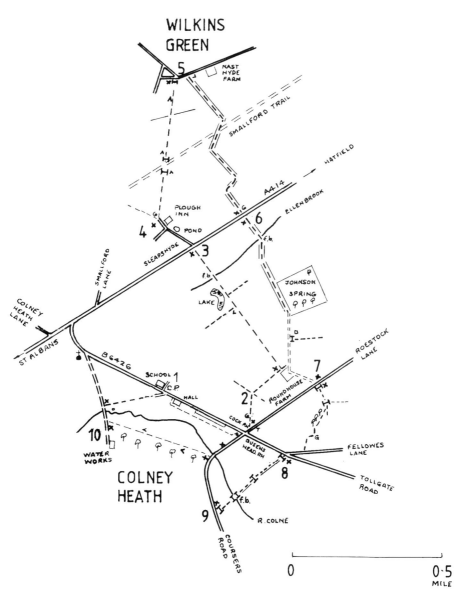

WILKINS
GREEN

NAST
HYDE
FARM

SMALLFORD TRAIL

HATFIELD

AA14

ELLENBROOK

PLOUGH
INN

4 POND

SLEAPSHYDE

SMALLFORD
LANE

COLNEY
HEATH
LANE

ST ALBANS

B6426

3

f.b.

LAKE

JOHNSON
SPRING

D

ROESTOCK
LANE

SCHOOL 1
C.P.

HALL

COCK P.H.

ROUNDHOUSE
FARM

2

7

10

WATER
WORKS

COLNEY
HEATH

QUEENS
HEAD P.H.

FELLOWES
LANE

8

TOLLGATE
ROAD

9

f.b.

R. COLNE

COURSERS
ROAD

0   0·5
                                    MILE

Total distance 4.5 miles (7.2km)

COLNEY HEATH AND WILKINS GREEN

Park in public car park next to Colney Heath School.
G.R. 201,061

1 From the car park turn L along the High Street (SE) passing Scholars Court R. Turn R at Village Hall, then L along grassy track parallel with road (SE). Continue along rear of housing to large white coal post, rejoin road near crossroads. Cross and turn L at the Queens Head P.H. along Roestock Lane for a few metres, to a signposted gap between housing opposite a telephone box. Go L (N) through this and a gate to a gap between metal posts at a junction of power lines. Take the clear path (N) diagonally across the field through two more posts.

2 At a clear crossing of paths turn half R and continue (NE) across a field. Soon is a hedge R then a junction of bridleways at a signpost. Here turn sharp L (NW) along a gravel track with hedge R. Soon this track becomes fenced on both sides and passes a small lake L.

3 At the junction with the A414, cross with care to Sleapshyde Lane. Continue through Sleapshyde to the Plough P.H. R. Go through the gap at the side of an iron gate (N).

4 Here ignore the path L, instead take the path half R due N across the field, This crosses the 'Smallford Trail' and continues (N) across another field to Wilkins Green.

5 Turn R along the lane (E) and after a few metres turn R into a hedged bridleway (SE). Recross the 'Smallford Trail' and continue to the A414 at a gate. This may be muddy in wet weather.

6 Cross over and continue (SE). Go past a wood L at the corner of which the track becomes a road which passes Roundhouse Farm, and meets Roestock Lane at Cherry Green Trees.

7 Cross the road, and the stile opposite (S) to another stile at the edge of trees. Turn half R across the playing field, along a row of trees. Go through an iron gate and turn L between two blocks of flats to meet Fellowes Lane. Turn R along this to the junction with Tollgate Road, and cross to the stile opposite.

8 Continue (SW) along a clear path with hedge L over two more stiles. Cross the river Colne at the footbridge, and the next stile into Coursers Road.

9 Turn R (N) along the road and at the bend turn L (NW) at a waymark sign. This pleasant path across the Heath with the river R and trees L meets an access road.

0 Turn R (N) noting the coal post on the right, cross the Colne river and immediately turn R again (E) on a path through trees leading to housing and the High Street. Cross over to the car park.

WALK 19

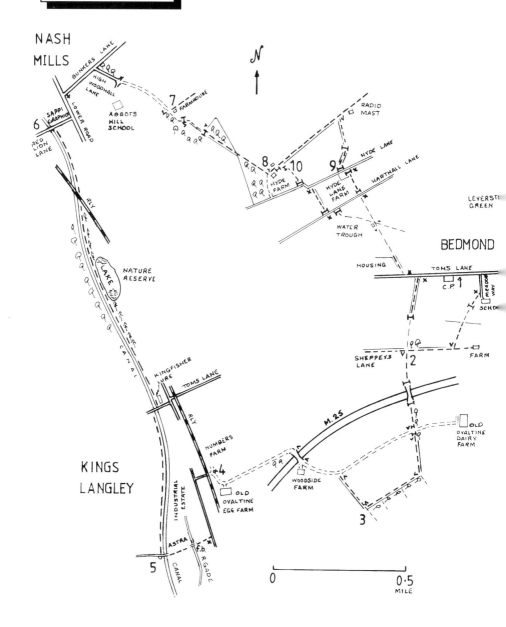

© Crown copyright

Total distance 6.3 miles (10.1km), or by the alternative route 6 miles (9.6km)

BEDMOND, KINGS LANGLEY AND NASH MILLS

Park in Recreation Area, Playing Fields, Toms Lane, Bedmond. G.R. 096,035.

1 From the car park, turn L down Toms Lane. At the signpost by number 190, turn L (S) into a path with fence R and hedge L. Continue (S) through another gap and stile across a field to a waymark in Sheppeys Lane.

2 Cross this track, continue (S) over another field to a footbridge over the M25 which has a stile at each end. Continue forward (S) crossing the farm access road, to another crossing path. Turn R (SW) along this path along the boundary of housing L with a field R.

3 At the next crossing path turn R (NW). This path with fence L meets the same access road crossed in Item 2. Bear L along this road passing on L a farmhouse 'Woodside' to a vehicle bridge over the M25 again. Continue along this road (W) passing the old Ovaltine Egg Farm L, go downhill to a T-junction with a farm track.

4 Turn L (SW) under the railway bridge where a short road leads to a T-junction with the Kings Langley road. Turn L (SE) along this road passing an industrial trading estate R. At the boundary of this estate, turn R along a fenced path (SW). Cross the river Gade by the bridge, continue along the boundary fence, and cross the canal by a second bridge.

5 Turn L, go under the bridge and continue along the towpath (N). At the next bridge in Toms Lane, cross the canal, turn L passing the housing Kingfisher Lure, on to the towpath (N). This pleasant path continues (N) past a lake, and under the railway bridge to Red Lion Lane.

6 Turn R in this Lane (E). At the junction with Lower Road turn L (N) towards Nash Mills. Take the next turning R (E) which is Bunkers Lane by a flint wall R. Take the next turning R, High Woodhall Lane which is a pleasant tree lined road. Go past Abbot's Hill School entrance R, and continue along an access road uphill (SE). This leads to a large farmhouse. Ignore the track L, instead turn R into a small copse.

7 This path continues (SE) along the boundary of the farmhouse to a stile. Cross this and continue downhill alongside a hedge R (SE). Cross another stile in a woodland fence and continue (SE) uphill through this wood and into a field path with hedge R leading to Hyde Farm.

8 Do not enter the farm, turn L along a clear track past a metal barn L. This soon becomes a field path leading to a radio mast (NE). Turn R at the waymark about 200m before reaching the mast along a fenced track (S), cross two stiles into Hyde Lane.

9 Turn L in this lane, and in a few metres turn R over a stile along the side of Hyde Lane Farm. This fenced path leads (SE) into Harthall Lane. Cross the lane to another stile and field path (SE). This leads to a water trough at the intersection of two paths. Continue (SE) to a gap near housing. A fenced path continues (SE) along the boundary of housing R to a gap in Toms Lane. Turn L up Toms Lane to the car park R.

0 **Alternatively:** at item 8 turn R at the metal barn cross the stile next to the gate, then another immediately L into a field. Continue (SE) to a stile in the hedge corner and cross into Hyde Lane. Go L along this lane for a few metres, turn R at a signposted track with hedge L (SE) into Harthall Lane. In a few metres L cross a stile where a path leads to the water trough item 9.

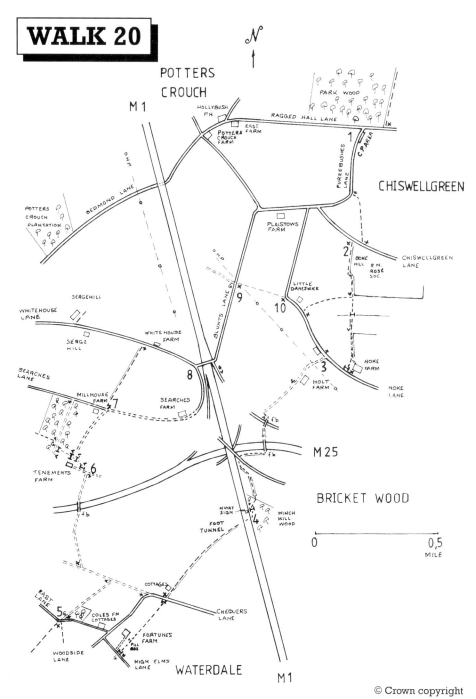

WALK 20

POTTERS CROUCH

CHISWELLGREEN

M25

BRICKET WOOD

WATERDALE

0   0,5 MILE

© Crown copyright

Total distance 6.5 miles (10.5km), only slightly longer by the alternative route

POTTERS CROUCH AND MOTORWAY INTERCHANGE

Parking is available on E side of Furzebushes Lane near junction with Ragged Hall Lane G.R. 127.051.

1 Walk down Furzebushes Lane (S) and in about 350m, where the lane bears R at the signpost, take the path ahead (S) across the field towards the footpath signpost in front of the large house. Cross the stile into Chiswell Green Lane, turn R go past the entrance to Bone Hill, the R.N. Rose Society L.

2 Turn L (S) at the signpost, and go along the boundary fence L of Bone Hill. At the waymark continue ahead (S) and cross the stile in the hedge. Continue (S) into a farm track with hedge L towards Noke Farm. Bear R (SW) in front of this farm (L) to a stile and signpost in Noke Lane. Turn R along this lane, and after 100m at a R bend, turn L along a bridleway marked 'private road'.

3 This track passes Holt Farm L and continues (SW) to a motorway boundary fence. A short L and R along a path with chain link fence on each side, leads to a footbridge over a feeder road. Continue (S) down steps to a second bridge over the M25 where there is a good view of the M25/M1 interchange. The path continues R between chain link under another feeder road bridge. At the end of the fencing, continue (S) through Winch Hill Wood to the M1 boundary fence. Cross the stile near the motorway sign, go down the steps to a foot tunnel under the M1.

4 On emerging from the tunnel, continue (SW) along a clear path with hedge L. Ignore a track L, and continue to Chequers Lane at Oaklea Cottages R. Cross the lane to a signposted stile opposite. Continue across a field (SW) passing Fortunes Farm R. Go past the pill box R (SW) to a stile in High Elms Lane. Then turn R along the asphalt track parallel with the lane. At the junction turn R along Woodside Lane. In a few metres turn L (W) into East Lane past Coles Farm Cottages.

5 The lane turns sharp L then R. At the signpost, go sharp R through a gate into a bridleway (NE) with small copse R. In about 350m at a transverse bridleway turn L (W) at a waymark. At the signposted fork bear R (N) along a gravel bridleway leading to a vehicle bridge over the M25. Cross this continue (N) to a crossing track leading to Tenements Farm L.

6 Do not enter the farm, look for a waymarked stile R and cross into a meadow. Turn L (NW) keep to a hedge L and in 150 metres cross a stile into the farm access road. Another stile opposite leads to a pleasant meadow with woods ahead. Continue (NW) between two large oaks with belt of trees L, go up the slope to a stile in the trees not easily seen. Cross and go straight ahead along a wide track in the woods (N). This meets Searches Lane along which turn R (E) to Millhouse Farm.

7 Continue (E) along this lane now only a grassy track, go past Searches Farm L, into the access road adjacent to the motorway R to the bridge in Blunts Lane.

Alternatively in wet weather at the signpost opposite Millhouse Farm, take the gravel track (NE) with hedge L into Whitehouse Lane. Turn R past Whitehouse Farm L to this bridge.

8 Turn R over the bridge across the many feeder lanes at this junction. Continue (NE) along this lane to the O.H. power line.

9 Here turn R (E) at the signpost along a grass path, across a field to a signpost just to L of a large house in Noke Lane.

10 Turn R (SE) in this lane past 'Little Daneswick'. In a few metres turn L (NE) at a signpost uphill to the corner of the boundary fence of Bone Hill. Turn L alongside this fence (N) into Chiswell Green Lane item 2. Turn L along the lane, then R along Furzebushes lane to the start of the walk.

Alternatively at item 9, continue along Blunts Lane (NE), turn L at Bedmond Lane (NW), then at Crouch Farm R to the Hollybush P.H. Here a R turn along Ragged Hall Lane (E) also leads to the start of the walk.

WALK 21

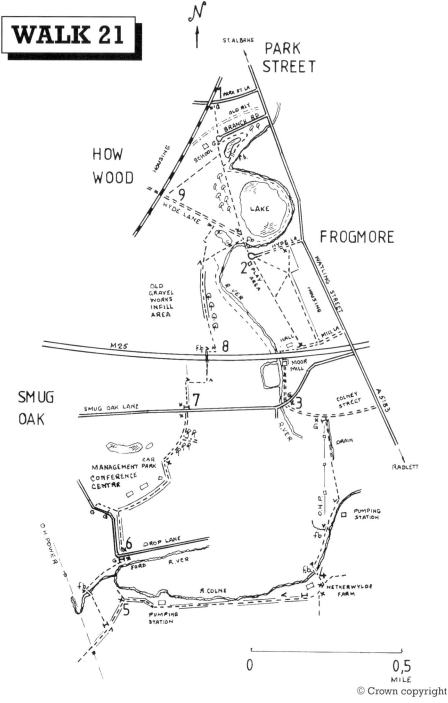

© Crown copyright

Total distance 5 miles (8.05km) with few stiles to cross.

PARK STREET, RIVERS VER AND COLNE

Park in Park Street Lane, Park Street, near playing field.
G.R. 148,039

1 Enter the playing field at the gate near the railway bridge, take the asphalt path, passing the children's play area R (SE). Go through the gap in the old disused railway, cross Branch Road and pass the school entrance R. Go through the gate opposite into the wide gravel track (S). Here a small diversion is worth trying. Immediately turn L, with lake R on a path which meets the river Ver (E). Turn R between the river and the lake, cross a small stream by the footbridge then the path rejoins the original gravel track. Turn L along this track continue (SE) passing a plantation R. This goes between two lakes, passes a signpost R and crosses the river by a steel footbridge at the end of Hyde Lane.

2 Go straight ahead (SE) across the infill area. Emerge through an iron gate into Mill Lane near the river. Turn R and take the gravel track between fences at the signpost near Hall and Co. Continue under the motorway bridge along the river bank to Moor Mill. The path continues with a short L and R round the mill into the access road and an iron gate.

3 Cross Smug Oak Lane into the bridleway opposite at the signpost. Take this gravel track (E) soon is a signpost and gate with a stile nearby. Cross this stile and go due S with power line R. This continues with a drain L and the pumping station ahead. At the bank of the river turn R along it. At a power line post carrying a junction of wires is a footbridge. Cross this and continue with river L and power line R towards the group of buildings Netherwylde Farm. Before reaching the farm turn L over a new bridge over the river Colne.

4 Go through a small avenue of trees to the signpost on a transverse bridleway. Turn R (W) go past Netherwylde Farm, ignore a turning L, at the signpost continue W along FP20. This is a firm wide track with views of the river R. Go past the pumping station R, and follow the wire fence R (W).

5 At the wooden signpost ignore the turning R, and continue SW on the bridleway towards the power lines. Before reaching the lines a path goes sharp R (NW) over a stile towards the river. Take this clear path, cross the river by the steel bridge, and turn R (NE) along the far bank noting the confluence of the rivers Ver and Colne.

6 Cross the stile into Drop Lane and cross to the gravel footpath and bridleway opposite. Go N along this with hedge L to the boundary fence of a Management and Conference Centre. Follow this fence L (NE) past the centre, and the small cemetery L, to the signpost by the car park. Continue R (NE) along the access road, ignore the turning R, go through the strip of woodland (N). Continue along the road to Smug Oak Lane.

7 Cross this lane with care and the signposted stile opposite. Continue (N) with wire fence R. After 100m turn R (E) through a waymarked gap in this fence into the infill area. In 200m at another waymark turn L (N) ascend the steps and cross the footbridge over the M25. On the far side turn R (E) for a few metres to a waymark post..

8 Turn L at this post and continue (N) with spinney and wire fence R. Eventually this path continues N between wire fences with views over lakes in the old sand quarry. In about 1km the path makes a short L and R with a good view over the last lake. Go through a gap in the hedge at the waymark, and turn L (W) along Hyde Lane. This goes for about 400m between hedges to a crossing over the railway.

9 Do not cross the railway, but instead turn sharp R (NE) along a clear path just before the railway. This goes along a school boundary (L) and emerges on to the original track in which turn L. Go through the gate into Branch Road, continue NW across the playing fields to the start of the walk.

WALK 22

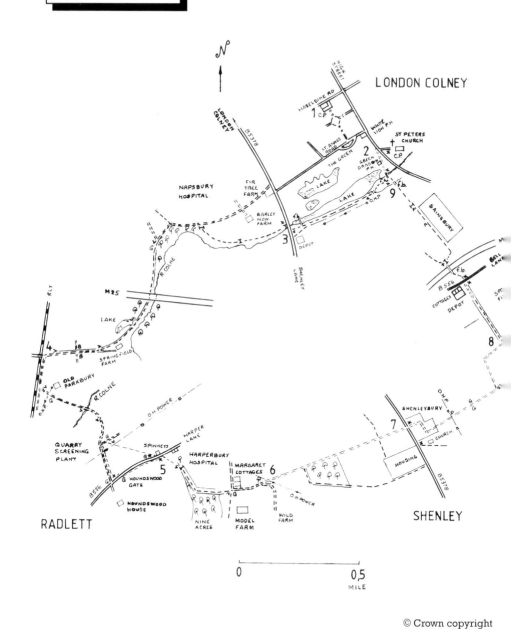

Total distance 6.5miles (10.5km).
Using the car park by St Peters Church, 5.7 miles (9.2km).

LONDON COLNEY, OLD PARKBURY AND SHENLEYBURY

WALK 22

Park in public car park in Haseldine, Road, London Colney.
G.R. 177,041 or by St Peters Church. G.R. 182,037

1 Take the asphalt path between housing at rear of car park (SE). Go through the circle of housing to the path opposite (SE) which leads to Sanders Close, Where this meets The Green, turn L along St. Annes Road (NE). At the White Lion P.H. turn R into the High Street. Bear R before the bridge, go past the Green Dragon P.H. R. (If using the St. Peters car park, cross the High Street to the Green Dragon P.H. opposite).

2 Turn L and cross the river by the footbridge. Then turn R at the signpost along a grassy path (W) alongside a hedge and Broad Colney lake R, and a fence and power line L. At the fork in the path ignore the track L, and continue (W) by the lake past the footbridge R, into Shenley Lane.

3 Turn R along the lane, and cross to the signposted stile down steps. The path now goes (W) along the N bank of the river, with wire fence L. Cross a stile into the bridleway and turn L. Note Napsbury Hospital R. Continue (W) on firm gravel surface, with copse L and views of the river L. Where the track turns sharp R, continue ahead (S) along a headland path with fence L overlooking the river. Continue (S) along the river bank under the M25 bridge. On emerging from the bridge, continue (SW) between fences passing a lake R and Springfield Farm L. Continue (W) along the farm access road to the railway bridge.

4 Do not cross the railway, instead turn L along the asphalt road (S) at the side of the railway R. Soon turn L at the waymark under power lines along the access road past Old Parkbury L (SE). Cross the river, and go past the quarry workings R. Look out for heavy vehicles, and continue (S) along the bridleway parallel to the access road. Turn L at the gate entrance and cross Harper Lane opposite Houndswood Gate. Continue along the asphalt path (NE) uphill to the signpost opposite the house 'Spinneys'.

5 Go through the gap in the fence and continue along a clear path (SE) towards a strip of woodland. Cross a stile, turn sharp R (SE) into a woodland strip alongside a wire fence R. Ignore a crossing track, continue (E) between wire fences and emerge on to an access road at Margaret Cottages. Continue (E) passing the disused Farm R. Avoid the fork R leading to Wild Farm instead take the clear track L up a slope (NE) on to open heath land passing under a power line.

6 Continue (NE) along the track past a wood R into Shenley Lane B5378. An alternative route around the wood and housing is shown on the opposite map.

7 Cross this road into Shenleybury Farm along a wide asphalt bridleway (NE) which soon makes a short R and L and continues as a clinker track through a gate. This wide track between hedges turns sharp L by a locked gate, followed by a R turn (NE).

8 At a transverse path marked by metal posts, turn L (NW) along a path with fence L and hedge R bordering a sports field. Continue into an access road passing a Works entrance and cottages L. This meets the B556 Bell Lane. Cross the lane to the track opposite which leads to a footbridge over the M25. At the far side cross the stile R to the boundary fence of Sainsbury R. Turn L (NW) and follow this fence to a stile at the far corner. Cross this, continue (NW) passing a small plantation R. Cross the river at the signposted footbridge.

9 Turn R past the Green Dragon P.H. to join the start of the walk item 2. Return along the High Street (NW) back to the car park.

WALK 23

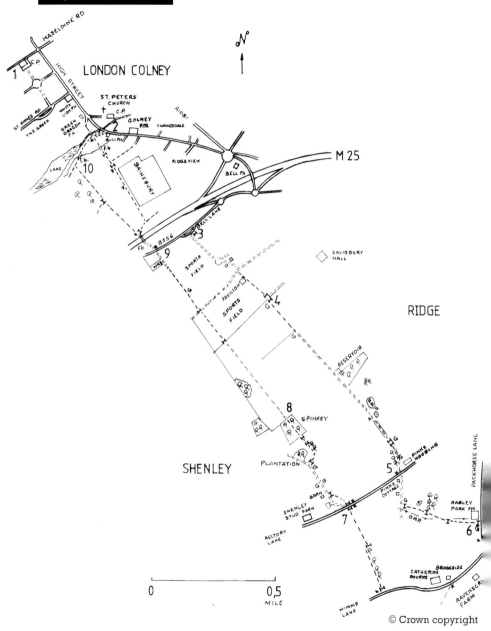

© Crown copyright

**Total distance 6.2 miles (10km) or by the alternative route 5.2 miles (8.4km).
Using the car park by St Peters Church 5.5 miles (8.8km) or 4.5 miles (7.2km).**

54

LONDON COLNEY, RIDGE AND SHENLEY

Park in public car park in Haseldine Road, London Colney.
G.R. 177,041 or in car park by St. Peters Church G.R. 182,037
at item 2.

1 Take the asphalt path between the housing at rear of car park (SE). Go through the circle of houses to the path opposite (SE) which leads to Sanders Close. Where this meets The Green, turn L along St. Annes Road (NE). At the White Lion P.H. turn R into the High Street. Continue (SE) then bear R before the bridge to the Green Dragon P.H. (If using the car park at St. Peters Church, cross the High Street to the Green Dragon P.H.)

2 Turn L (SE) and cross the river by the footbridge. Cross a small brook, and continue (SE) with a small plantation L. Cross a stile to meet the Sainsbury boundary fence L (SE). Continue past the waymark L to the corner of the fence. Bear R to a stile and signpost leading to the footbridge over the M25. Cross this into the gravel track which meets Bell Lane. Turn L (NE) along the lane for 100m.

3 At the University College Hospital London Sports Ground entrance, turn R through gates and go along the concrete access road to the turning circle. Bear R along a concrete track (SE) passing a house R, with ditch and hedge L. A short R and L leads to a transverse bridleway. Cross this, go behind the pavilion R and continue (SE) with hedge L. Cross a stile to another transverse track. Note Salisbury Hall L.

4 Go past a farm gate R, and continue ahead along a wide cinder track over fields (SE) towards a wood. This track becomes a concrete access road passing the wood L, then crosses a field (SE) with a small group of trees L to a gap with a waymark. Continue into a grassy path with hedge L and wire fence R. Cross two stiles near a gate L and continue along a wide grass track between hedges. This emerges on to Rectory Lane at a signpost by Pinks Farm Housing.

5 Turn L along the lane, and in a few metres R along an asphalt access road (S) passing Pinks Cottage R. Just before the road turns L, and at a O.H. power line turn L, cross a stile by a gate, and continue (E) under the power line. Pass a small pond L, and in the corner of a wood L cross another stile by a gate. Continue E with hedge L, cross a third stile, then with Rabley Park Farm L, cross a fourth stile into Packhorse Lane.

6 Turn R along the lane (S) past Rabley Park L, and Rabley Willow R. Where the road bears L, keep straight on along a short path into Mimms Lane, into which turn R. Continue (SW) past Ravenscroft Farm L, and Catherine Bourne Farm R. In a further 250m is a stile and signpost R (FP 18). Cross this into a meadow with a row of trees R (NW). Continue with fence R over a stile to another by a gate into Rectory Lane.

7 Cross the stile and the lane, to the stile opposite into a meadow. Follow the wooden fence L by the farm access road, and when this bears R look for another stile by the large barn. Cross this into a wide access road with a wooden fence on each side. Go downhill (NW) passing gates on each side to a stile with gate R near a small plantation. Cross this and go diagonally to a fence and row of trees R. Continue to a stile in a transverse fence and hedge, cross into a small field, cross another stile ahead into a small spinney. At the far boundary, emerge into farmland.

8 Looking NW towards the Sainsbury, note a gap in the hedge in the distance. Go straight across the field, passing a hollow L and go through this gap (NW). Cross a small field and continue (NW) into an access road with Works entrance and cottages L. Cross Bell Lane.

9 Go along the gravel track and cross the same footbridge as in item 2. On the other side do not cross the stile, instead continue (NW) along a track with hedge L. Ignore a path L, and after passing a small copse L, meet a transverse path by a lake.

0 Here turn R (NE) and with lake L, cross a small footbridge meeting the original path at the Colne footbridge signpost. Cross the steel bridge, turn R to the Green Dragon P.H. Turn L, go up the High Street and so back to the car park.

Alternatively to shorten the walk, at item 5, Pinks Farm Housing, turn R along Rectory Lane (SW) to item 7 at Stud Farm.

WALK 24

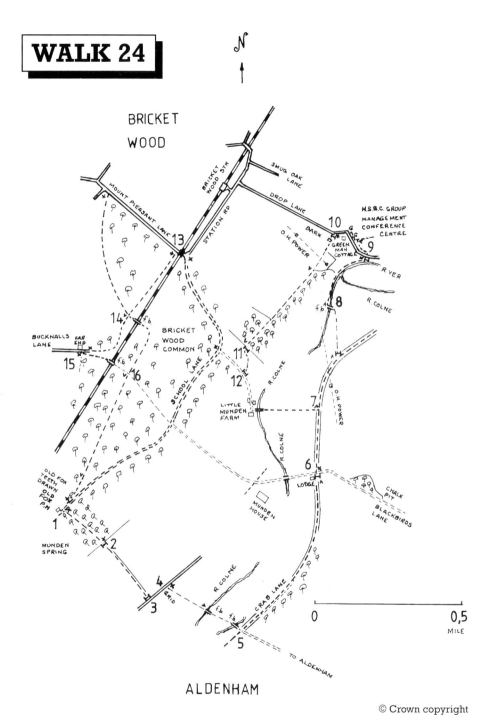

N

BRICKET
WOOD

ALDENHAM

© Crown copyright

Total distance 5 miles (8.1km), or using the shorter route 4 miles (6.4km).

COLNE VALLEY AND BRICKETWOOD

Park in School Lane, Bricket Wood near The Old Fox public
house. G.R. 126,003

1 From The Old Fox go a few metres N and turn R onto a clear path (SE) through the woods.

2 At the boundary fence cross the stile, continue straight on (SE) with fence L.

3 Cross another stile, and turn L along the access road leading to Munden Home.

4 Immediately after crossing a cattle grid, turn R along a grassy path (SE). This continues over a field to a footbridge over the river Colne, and a second bridge over a flood stream usually dry.

5 In a few metres, at the junction of tracks, turn L (NE) along Crab Lane. Further on note Munden House L.

6 At the Lodge house, turn R along Blackbirds Lane for a diversion to an old chalk pit in a copse L where children can play. Returning to the Lodge, the track continues (N) between hedges. Note Little Munden Farm L.

7 Continue (N) passing under the power lines. After a further 100m, when the bridleway turns (NE), our path turns L (N) to a footbridge over the river Colne.

8 Cross the bridge, and turn R along the river bank. After a few metres note the confluence of the rivers Ver and Colne. Continue (N) into Drop Lane.

9 Cross this lane to a bridle path opposite which goes (NE). Where this turns R, a path leads off L at an iron pipe rail. This follows the boundary of the gardens of H.S.B.C. Group Management and Conference Centre. Ignore the first gate L, and go through the second gate L into Drop Lane. Turn R up the lane (W) and at a bend by Green Man Cottage is a stile L. Cross this to an old barn.

10 The path goes to the L of this barn and continues with a fence L (SW). The path leads to a field and crosses it to the corner of the woodland opposite, Continue (SW) along the edge of the wood L then through a small plantation to a stile in the boundary fence.

1 Cross this stile, and the meadow (S) to another stile on to the access road to Little Munden Farm.

2 Turn R (NW) along this road which is a public right of way. At the junction with School Lane turn R (NW). This is a pleasant wooded lane with little traffic.

3 This leads to Mount Pleasant Lane in which turn L, go under the railway bridge, and immediately turn L along a path (SW) which follows the railway boundary fence L.

4 Ignore a crossing path, continue ahead with chain link fence R. The path curves (W) and continues into an asphalt road, Bucknalls Lane.

5 Opposite a house named Far End, another path joins acutely sharp L (SE). Re-enter the woods along this path, keep to the boundary fence L, and cross the railway footbridge. Continue for about 100m.

6 At a clearing and a crossing of paths, turn R (SW) and continue through the woods, passing a cottage called 'Old Fox with its teeth drawn`. Go through the gap in the railing on to The Old Fox P.H. the start of the walk.

Alternatively if starting from Bricket Wood Station, go down Station Road (SW) and start the walk at item 13, return to the station after item 12.

A shorter walk can be devised by turning L at item 7 (SW) along a wide farm track. Cross the concrete bridge at Little Munden Farm, turn R along the access road (N) and rejoin the above route at item 12.

PLACES OF INTEREST

item number in text

HYDE MILL, BOWER HEATH AND BATFORD

WALK 1

1. **LEA VALLEY WALK** originally Great Northern Branch Railway which ran from Hatfield, Welwyn, Wheathampstead, Harpenden, Chiltern Green, Luton and Dunstable.
RED COW P.H. C16/17 timber framed core, C18 red brick front, extended in C20 at rear.

6. **HOLCROFTS SPRING WOOD** small area of woodland with public path round perimeter, managed by Hertfordshire Countryside Management Service.

8. **THE THATCHED COTTAGE** Crabtree Lane, C17 with exposed timber frame, red brick infill, modified 1930. Note deep thatched roof and porch hood.

WHEATHAMPSTEAD, BATFORD AND MACKERYE END

WALK 2

1. **THE BULL P.H.** a range of half-timbered buildings, early C16, with early C17 additions. Tall C17 central stack, open fireplaces with finely moulded surroundings.

3. **LEASEY BRIDGE FARM** see Walk 6, item 5.

4. **MARQUIS OF GRANBY P.H.** C17 timber framed, roughcast, ridge stack, C17/C18 single storey wings.

5. **MACKERYE END** c1665 timber framed house, mid C19 gabled addition, large red brick stack, c1700 moulded fireplace on first floor, 1665 open well staircase. Known to Charles Lamb, see 'Mackerye End' in Essays of Elia.

7. **TURNERS HALL FARM** C16 and C17 house, refaced C19 in flint and redbrick. Cross wing c1500 has a king strut roof.
THE SLYPE 'Hogs Island' Blackmore End C16 house, moved from St. Ippollitts 1928.

8. **TIN POT P.H.** C15 or early C16 origins, exposed C16 timber frame at rear wing. Main front is C18 red brick casing.
GUSTARD WOOD COMMON numbers 3,6,8,9,10,17 are all C17 or C18 timber framed.
HERONS FARM early C16 timber framed with C18 red brick casing, and king strut roof. Originally a close studded range of 4 bays N wing C16 probably a bakehouse. Barn C17.
THE DELL C18 house, timber framed, brick base, black weatherboarding, original central ridge stack.

11. **ST. HELENS** Wheathampstead Parish Church, mentioned in Domesday Book as Watamstede, C14 largely unchanged since then. Splendid 'Broach' spire, tower c1290. Garrard memorial c1700, floor brasses c1450, alabaster tomb chest of Sir John Brocket 1558. Well worth a visit.

GUSTARD WOOD AND LAMER PARK

WALK 3

1. **CORN MILL** over river Lea C16/17 timber framed mill, cased 1890-5 now a warehouse .

3. **GUELDERS** C18 wing on R,1840 main block in yellow gault brick, weatherboarded upper floor.

4. **LAMER HILL GATE** house C17 timber framed, cased in red brick C18, L-shaped, C20 extension.

58

REDBOURN AND FLAMSTEAD

1. **CRICKET PAVILION** Redbourn Common is used by the local cricket club, the oldest known local team in the country, dating from 1666. Matches played here every weekend in the season.

5. **NICHOLLS FARM** C16 or earlier, recased and extended C17, chequered red brick, interior C16 beams and inglenook, S end is C17 outhouse.

ROTHAMSTED AND HARPENDENBURY

4. **ROTHAMSTED MANOR HOUSE** A large imposing red brick mansion mainly 1630 to 1650 incorporating an earlier medieval dwelling, now a hall of residence. The front on S has mullioned and transomed window casements, a three storied porch with Gothic cupola, and Dutch gables. The hall has linenfold panelling c1550. Stone fireplaces with Jacobean. chimney piece. Complete set of late C16 early C17 wall paintings behind panelling. Extended for Sir John Bennett Lawes 1863.
NICKY LINE. This railway ran from Harpenden, through Redbourn, to Hemel Hempstead, opened in 1877. Passenger service withdrawn 1947 due to post-war coal shortage, reopened 1968 by Claydales for transport of Hemelite blocks, Now a footpath called the 'Nicky Line'.

5. **HARPENDENBURY** Farmhouse C15 or early C16 hall house, extended by three bays on S late C17, cross wing mid C19, rear wall has Wealden framing, large central C17 ridge stack. Note the C15 early C16 Tithe barn.

9. **THE OLD HOUSE** 27 Leyton Road, late C16 known as Bull Inn, late C17 early C18 extension, timber frame exposed at rear, roughcast with brick nogging. C17 stack, wide inglenooks, well preserved house.
COACH LANE COTTAGE C15 and later, timber framed house on L plan, C17 inserted red brick stack.
ROTHAMSTED MEMORIAL see walk 8, item 1.
WEST COMMON see walk 8, item 1.
FLOWTON PRIORY see walk 8, item 1.
WHITE HORSE P.H. see walk 8, item 7.

NOMANSLAND, HARPENDEN AND WHEATHAMPSTEAD

1. **WEST END FARM** late C17 with early C19 front range, red brick C19 granary at N end. Two barns C18 or early C19 timber framed.

4. **ALDWICKBURY FARM**, granary mid C18 red brick, weatherboarded cupola, upper floor has jettied balcony.

5. **LEA VALLEY WALK** see walk 1, item 1.
LEASEY BRIDGE FARM originally a C16 timber framed house with C17 extension, red brick chimney. Single storey bay R probably a former hall, open well staircase 1665.

7. **OLD SCHOOL** built 1869, now offices. Polychrome decorated Gothic style, knapped flint walling in zig-zag bonds of yellow gault brick, wooden belfry with leaded spike, dog tooth eaves.

REDBOURN AND REDBOURNBURY

1. **OLD SCHOOL** Redbourn Common is now used as offices.
CUMBERLAND HOUSE large Georgian red brick house 1745, Roman Doric doorcase, C18 stacks, well preserved interior, was once a shooting lodge of Duke of Cumberland.
HIGH STREET AND FISH STREET many interesting C16 and C17 houses and shops.
NICKY LINE see walk 5, item 4.

3. **HAMMONDS END HOUSE** c1700 dark red brick, 3 storeys, large inglenook in kitchen.

5. **REDBOURNBURY** farmhouse, originally a manor. house, C15 hall, extended in mid C16 and C17, fine braced arch roof on stone corbels, C17 gabled stair turret at rear, and service wing.
REDBOURNBURY MILL mid C18 extended on W early C19, chequered and plain red brick, mill block has 2 storey stack hoist, some mill mechanism intact. Disastrous fire August 87, mill now rebuilt.

7. **DOLITTLE MILL** C17 half timbered, whitewashed building, C17 stack, C18 sash windows. Adjacent barn C18 early C19, has exposed timber frame.
CHEQUERS P.H. late C16 early C17 timber framed, painted brick casing, C18/C19 N bay rebuilt, C19/C20 rear extension. Was once part of Fish Street Farm property of Lord Verulam.

HARPENDEN AND HAMMONDS END

1. **ROTHAMSTED MEMORIAL STONE** commemorates 50 years of continuous experiments in agriculture, the first of their kind, by Sir John Bennett Lawes and Joseph Henry Gilbert: 1843/93.
WEST COMMON numbers 15, 16 cottage terrace, C17/C18 timber framed core, late C18 red brick casing, N gable and exposed frame, C18 external stack.
FLOWTON PRIORY early C16 Priory, timber framed, C20 red brick nogging, leaded casements throughout, C16 stone fireplaces, some C16 stained glass, late C17 staircase. Building moved from Ipswich 1925, sold in 1933.

4. **HAMMONDS END HOUSE** see walk 7, item 3.

6. **HATCHING GREEN** number 1 thatched cottage, late C17 early C18 timber framed with red brick casing, restored C20, external stack.

7. **WHITE HORSE P.H.** C17 rear wing, front range probably earlier, timber framed, C18 red brick nogging, C18 ridge stack,

NOMANSLAND, SYMONDSHYDE AND COLEMAN GREEN

1. **NOMANSLAND** so named because it was the boundary between lands owned by St. Albans and Westminster Abbeys.
NOMANSLAND FARM front range c1705, extended at rear c1800, red brick, front has c1800 sash windows. Barns C18 timber framed.

4. **SYMONDSHYDE FARM** farmhouse C17 timber framed, C19 red brick extensions, C17 cross wing.

7. **JOHN BUNYAN'S CHIMNEY.** Remains of stack of cottage where John Bunyan sometimes preached, see commemorative plaque. Cottage mid C17 enlarged in C18, timber bressumer visible. Enclosed in small public garden.

8. **OLD BEECH HYDE HOUSE** late C15 hall house, mid C17 cross wing, cased in red brick, large external mid C17 stack, C16 floor beams, 1980 extension on W, connects with C19 barn range.

9. **BEECH HYDE FARM** C16 hall house, T shaped in plan, half timbered, brick faced, C17 ceilings, moulded beams, well preserved brick fireplaces, fine stacks.

REDBOURN TO
HOGG END LANE

WALK
10

1. **OLD SCHOOL** see walk 7, item 1.
   NICKY LINE see walk 5, item 4.

4. **HOGG END** farmhouse late C16, timber framed, large C17 wing on R, late C17 barn L.

5. **BUTLERS FARM** c1700, altered c1830, red brick house square plan, two ridge stacks. Interior has c1830 detail. Workshop on W is C17/C18.
   KETTLEWELL FARM early C17 half timbered, weatherboarded. Late C18 timber framed barn.
   OLD JEROMES late medieval, timber framed, probably open hall, c1600 stack and fireplaces inserted, bay added on E, C17/C18.

6. **SOUTHEND FARM** C17 and C18 half timbered, brick cased, C18/C19 rear extension, C17 stacks at rear.

8. **DANE END FARM** mid C18 or earlier red brick, with internal stacks at each end.
   FLOWERS FARM C17 timber framed, re-cased in red brick c1830, C19 extension on NW.

10. **ST. MARY** Redbourn Parish Church c1100 nave and W tower, c1140 N aisle, c1340 chancel, C15 brasses, C18/C19 monuments. Well worth a visit.
    CHURCH END number 2 formerly The Jolly Gardner P.H., C16 timber framed. Many other properties here are C17/C18.
    HOLLYBUSH P.H. C16, altered C17, timber framed, plastered front, exposed framing at rear, C18 brick infill.

1. **BAKERS FARM** now a house, C17 exposed timber frame, painted brick infill, rebuilt ridge stack.

BATCHWOOD AND CHILDWICK
GREEN

WALK
11

2. **BATCHWOOD HALL**, built c1800 by Lord Grimthorpe as a country seat from which he could view the Abbey.

4. **CHILDWICKBURY** late C17 built for Joshua Lomax, remodelled 1854, stucco on brick, Doric carriage entrance. Water tower on slate SE late C18 Gothic style red brick. Coach house and stable court c1890. Dairy late C19 for Sir John Blundell Maple.
   CHILDWICK GREEN Church of St. Mary and adjoining school, 1867 by Sir George Gilbert Scott, red brick, single aisle, Nos. 12 to 15 1890 red patterned brick, behind No. 15 is a loggia of the former 'One Bell' P.H. later a club house. Forge cottage late C17 timber framed house, later a red brick infill. Wellhead on green is late C19, cast iron winding gear is intact.

5. **CHILDWICK LODGE** 1897 lodge to Childwickbury, red brick and cream terracotta, Jacobean style, stair turrent with conical roof, mullioned casements, wrought iron gates.

WEST OF SANDRIDGE

5. **POUND FARM** late C15/C16, extended and altered C17/C18, timber framed, C18 staircase, C18 inserted stack. Two barns, one C15/16, the other C16/17.

6. **QUEEN'S HEAD P.H.** 3 dormer single storey, timber framed building C16/17, recased mid C19, weatherboarded.

3. **ST. LEONARDS** Sandridge Parish Church, see walk 13, item 3.

7. **THREE HORSESHOES P.H.** built as 2 semi-detached cottages, C18, large inglenooks with original curved staircases at each end.

MARSHALSWICK, SANDRIDGE AND SYMONDSHYDE

3. **ST. LEONARDS** Sandridge Parish Church late C11 early C12, chancel is C14, restored in 1886, W end and tower rebuilt, chancel arch is C14 which retains the late C11 arch incorporating Roman brick. Two C19 monuments, worth a visit.

6. **FAIRFOLDS FARM** farmhouse C17, N front refaced in brick C18/C19.

7. **FAIRFOLDS FARM COTTAGES** Nos. 1, 2 Woodcock Hill, originally C15/16 timber framed farmhouse, cross wings C17, with C17 red brick ridge stack.
CAPS COTTAGES originally 3 cottages, mid C17, recased and extended both ends in late C18 early C19, now a house. C19 roughcast, dentilled brick eaves all round.

8. **NASHES FARM** late C17, recased in red brick 1888, timber framed, C17 staircase. Attached barn C15/16, probably the shell of an earlier farmhouse.

ST. MICHAELS, POTTERS CROUCH AND GORHAMBURY

1. **VERULAMIUM MUSEUM** has several fine Roman mosaics, pottery and other finds from nearby Roman City of Verulamium. In adjoining parkland is a hypocaust or suite of Roman baths.
GREBE HOUSE C16 timber framed building resited here, now home of Herts. and Middlesex Wildlife Trust.

2. **ROMAN WALL** part of the Verulamium boundary wall, note outline of base of massive E Gate, which is in line with Watling Street.

5. **EAST FARM** late C15 hall house, mainly C17 exterior, timber framed, crownpost roof, well preserved interior.
HOLLYBUSH P.H. C17 timber framed, roughcast, large brick stack on W, C19 2 storey extension on E.

6. **POTTERS CROUCH FARM** C17 half timbered with C18 brick facing.
APPSPOND LANE Nos. 1,2 C16/17, altered 1950. Appspond Cottage 1788, C17 oak panelling. The Cottage mid C17 exposed timber frame, C18 red brick casing.

7. **HILL END FARM** late medieval house, C18 brick cased, C17 plaster ceiling with fleur-de-lys on Tudor rose detail.
HILLEND COTTAGES c1600, half timbered walls, tall capped stacks.
TEMPLE COTTAGES mid C18 Palladian-style garden temple, late C19 extension at rear to form a cottage range, gable end crowned by ball finials and stone busts.
OLD GORHAMBURY began 1563 by Sir Nicholas Bacon, extended in red brick and flint, Ionic columns. Visited by Queen Elizabeth I.

GORHAMBURY began 1777 for 3rd Viscount Grimston, by architect Sir Robert Taylor, refaced in Portland stone in 1957-67, entrance has Corinthian portico. Interior has some fireplaces attributed to Piranesi, paintings of members of Bacon family.
DAIRY N of main building 1830, peristyle of cast iron colonettes.
NASH'S LODGE 1830-40 stucco, formerly a lodge to Gorhambury.
MAYNES FARMHOUSE late C17, refronted C19 in red brick. Barn C16,
ROMAN THEATRE the only visible Roman Theatre in Britain.

OAKLANDS, SMALLFORD AND SLEAPSHYDE

WALK 15

1. **HILL END HOSPITAL** built 1899 as the Hertfordshire County Asylum. St. Bartholomews Hospital based here in World War Two, returned to London during 1950s and 60s.
OAKLANDS COLLEGE main building was a house 1782, tower added 1844. Oaklands Park 335 acres including mansion, cottages, outbuildings, mill and reservoir, bought by Herts. C.C. 1920 for training of students of agriculture. New study bedrooms opened 1953. John Innes estate 240 acres at Bayfordbury incorporated in 1967, making total of 650 acres of arable and grass.

2. **OAK FARM HOUSE** C17 timber framed, C19/20 red brick ground floor, large red brick stack R, C17/18 external stack on L, C19 rear extensions. Blocked inglenook.

5. **THREE HORSESHOES P.H.** early C18 timber framed, plastered brick casing, C19 extensions L and rear, C20 extension R.

6. **PLOUGH INN** late C17 timber framed, painted brick ground floor, plastered upper, large external red brick stack, 1960 extension L, thatched roof.
SMALLFORD TRAIL site of old railway which ran from St. Albans Abbey station to Hatfield opened in 1865, closed to passengers 1951. Smallford station now used by scrap metal dealer. Smallford Trail is now a footpath and cycleway linking with Alban Way, see walk 16, item 2.

7. **COLNEY HEATH** originally about 200 acres and known as Tyttenhanger Heath, being owned by the Manor of Tyttenhanger. Early C12 manor given to St. Albans Abbey, when the Abbot then granted grazing rights to certain commoners.

VERULAMIUM, RIVER VER AND PARK STREET

WALK 16

1. **KINGSBURY MILL** C16 working mill on river Ver, loading door on first floor, and museum of mill machinery. Tea house adjacent to mill.
FIGHTING COCKS P.H. C16 octagonal 2-storey timber framed building with high pitched pointed roof, very heavy timbers internally, tall tapered external stack. One of the oldest inns in the country.

2. **SOPWELL NUNNERY** remains of C16 house is on the site of Sopwell Priory founded in 1140 by Geoffrey de Gorham for Benedictine nuns. Priory suppressed in 1537.
ALBAN WAY part of disused railway from St. Albans Abbey Station to Hatfield, closed 1951. Opened as a footpath and cycleway 1988, continuous with Smallford Trail. See walk 15, item 6.

3. **SOPWELL HOUSE HOTEL** C18 Georgian house, once the residence of the Mountbatten family. Originally belonged to Gorhambury.

4. **HEDGES FARM** C17 timber framed, C18 red brick cased, 1840 painted brick front, C17 stack.
TOLL COTTAGE C16/17 timber framed, with later alterations, wide stack over partly roofed brick bake oven with inglenook fireplace. Interior exposed beams.

item number in text **PARK MILL** on site of a mill built in timber 1185, rebuilt 1846 in red brick, corn grinding ceased 1913, it then became a glue factory. Mill house opposite renamed Corvill House. C18 overshot water wheel in basement visible to visitors. Mill rebuilt 1987. Now occupied by offices.

9. **ST. STEPHENS** Parish Church, founded in 948, built in flint c1100. Norman nave and N aisle incorporating Roman brick, C13 Lady Chapel, wood shingled spire.
KING HARRY P.H. mid C18 red brick, C19 hood over door.

LONDON COLNEY, RIVER COLNE AND COLNEY HEATH

WALK
17

2. **ST. PETERS** London Colney Parish Church 1825 Norman revival, single aisle, rear gallery, E window stained glass 1865.

4. **WOODRAKE COTTAGE** C17/18 timber framed, early C19 casing, weatherboarded, steep pitched roof,

7. **COAL POST** new Church Lane, 1861 to mark limit of coal duty area round London.

8. **TYTTENHANGER PARK** country house, now offices, built in c1655, altered early C18 and extended, red brick. On front ridge is a large square wooden clock turret surmounted by octagonal bell chamber with cupola. Interior Jacobean panelling, original main staircase to all 3 storeys, 2nd floor chapel, family paintings.

9. **THE BULL P.H.** see walk 23, item 2.

10. **TELFORDS BRIDGE?** 1774, thought now not to be by Telford, 7 arches.
WATERSIDE Colne House c1800, stucco porch with Ionic columns. Riverside cottage mid C19. Waterside House C18 timber framed.
HIGH STREET London Colney, Nos. 27,29,31,33, C17 timber framed, brick cased later.

COLNEY HEATH AND WILKINS GREEN

WALK
18

1. **COAL POST** on heath, near Queen's Head P.H., note City of London crest, this marked the limit of coal duty area round London.
QUEEN'S HEAD P.H. C17/18 timber framed, with C19/20 additions, C19 canted bay window on ground floor, said to have been used to collect coal tax, c1763 inglenook.

3. **SLEAPSHYDE** hamlet known as Slepes hide 1598. Ye old house nos. 1,2,3, C17, with C19/20 casing, C17 stack.
SLEAPSHYDE FARMHOUSE early C16 hall house, timber framed, floored late C17, massive central red brick stack, C 17/18 service extension with oven stack.
PLOUGH P.H. see walk 15, item 6.

4. **SMALLFORD TRAIL** see walk 15, item 6.

BEDMOND, KINGS LANGLEY AND NASH MILLS

2. **OVALTINE DAIRY FARM** 1932 black and white building, built as a copy of the dairy farm owned by Marie Antoinette in Versailles. Now converted to private dwellings named Antoinette Court.

9. **GRAND UNION CANAL** originally named the Grand Junction Canal, begun in 1792. Aylesbury branch opened in 1813, Chief Engineer William Jessop.

13. **HYDE FARM** mid C16 timber framed, extended C17, cased and extended C18, altered C19/20, C18 external stacks and staircase.

16. **HYDE LANE FARM** late C15 hall bay, timber framed, red brick cased, floored and heated C17, cross wing rebuilt 1977.

POTTERS CROUCH AND MOTORWAY INTERCHANGE

2. **BONE HILL** early Victorian house, on an earlier farm site, since been extended each end. Once the home of John Broadwood, piano manufacturer. Bought by Royal National Rose Society 1959, grounds extended 1964, now the principal rose garden in Britain, and of international fame.

3. **HOLT FARM** farmhouse, open hall C15, altered C16/17, extended at each end C18, timber framed, inserted floor, main beams c1600 of high quality, C17 barn.
WINCH HILL WOOD part of a triangular site between M25, MI, A405, now threatened by development.

5. **TENEMENTS FARM** C15 medieval hall house, rectangular plan, c1600 ceilings and stack, main stack is C17, oven stack C18. Original massive hall tie beam is visible internally.

6. **MILLHOUSE FARM** C16 timber framed, L-shaped, recased and extended late C18, C16/17 stacks and floor beams.

7. **SEARCHES FARM** C15/16 cruck framed farmhouse, C18 red brick cased, C17 central stack. Front sundial 1728.
WHITEHOUSE FARM C16 timber framed, 1788 brick front. Interior open fireplace, C18 staircase.

9. **DANESWICK** farmhouse C17 with exposed timber frame, central ridge stack. Inglenook formerly with staircase attached to stack.

PARK STREET, RIVERS VER AND COLNE

. **PARK STREET** after departure of Romans, area was known as the hamlet of Parkye.

. **MOOR MILL** mill house c1700, altered in C19, painted red brick ground floor, weatherboarded upper floor. Mill added in C19. 4 stable doors, sack hoist doors, with hoisting bay in roof.

. **NETHERWYLDE FARM** on site known as Netherwelde late C13, farmhouse C16/17 timber framed, central stack, S front is brick and flint. Interior has open fireplace with cast iron fireback having Arms of James I, and Jacobean wall painting. Two farm buildings have plaques early C18.

. **H.S.B.C. GROUP MANAGEMENT AND CONFERENCE CENTRE** was a farmhouse with late medieval front, C17 rear, with C19 additions, exposed timber frame, red brick infill, open hall, C17 staircase. known earlier as Hansteads, home of Lord and Lady Yule who bred Arab stallions for racing. Tomb of Lord David Yule is on the estate near the car park.

LONDON COLNEY, OLD PARKBURY AND SHENLEYBURY

WALK 22

1. **GREEN DRAGON P.H.** built as an inn early C17, timber framed, C18 rear extension, and red brick casing. Interior C17 panelling said to be from Salisbury Hall.

2. **BROAD COLNEY** lakes are a nature Reserve with much wildlife. Administered by Herts. and Middlesex Nature Conservancy Trust.

3. **NAPSBURY HOSPITAL** site including Manor Farm in 412 acres acquired in 1898 by Middlesex C.C. as County Asylum. Foundations laid in 1901, opened in 1905, having a rail siding with link to London. Used in World War One as a military hospital. Siding closed in 1959. New church built 1960.

4. **OLD PARKBURY** C15/16 timber framed farmhouse, early C19 casing. Late C17 lateral stack in yellow brick, roughcast rear elevation.

5. **HARPERBURY HOSPITAL** for the mentally handicapped, building commenced 1928, main building 1934, giving a pleasant aspect of separate villas and workshops. Site initially was Porters Park Estate, and used as an aerodrome in World War One. Known in 1930s as Middlesex Colony, renamed Harperbury in 1950.

6. **ST. BOTOLPHS** originally Parish Church of Shenleybury, built c1424, altered 1753. Original nave and S aisle remain. Made redundant 1972, now a private house. Nicholas Hawksmoor 1736-75 pupil of Wren, and who assisted in design of St. Pauls Cathedral, lies buried nearby.

LONDON COLNEY, RIDGE AND SHENLEY

WALK 23

2. **BULL P.H.** mid C16 timber framed with plastered walls, exposed frame at E end, c1900 canted sash window bays, C17/18 external stack. Inglenook in saloon bar was hidden behind four more recent fireplaces.

3. **SALISBURY HALL** 1668-79 with. C20 extensions, red brick with stone dressings. Interior has C17 oak panelling, house is surrounded by a moat. De Havilland Mosquito aircraft was designed here. Nell Gwyn Cottage, Old Coach House, granary and barns are all C17/18.

6. **RABLEY PARK FARM** C17, extended C18 timber framed, roughcast, kitchen bay added on L.

COLNE VALLEY AND BRICKET WOOD

WALK 24

1. **OLD FOX P.H.** mainly C19.

5. **MUNDEN HOUSE** 1787/95 in red brick, remodelled 1828 in stock brick with stone dressings. Interior has well preserved Victorian features. Recently the home of Lord Knutsford.

6. **LITTLE MUNDEN FARM** C17 half timbered farmhouse.

9. **GREEN MAN COTTAGE** C17 timber framed house with painted brick front, weatherboarded E gable, C18/19 stack.

15. **RAILWAY LINE** connects Watford junction, Garston, Bricket Wood, Park Street, and St. Albans Abbey stations. First opened 1858. Bricket Wood station opened 1862. Route now electrified 1988.

16. **OLD FOX WITH TEETH DRAWN** timber framed C17 cottage with thatched roof, lath and plaster wall. Typical Hertfordshire cottage of that period.

BIBLIOGRAPHY

HERTFORDSHIRE WALKS BOOKLETS

1. Afoot in Hertfordshire, D. Veall, Spurbooks Ltd., 1979.
2. Discovering Walks in Hertfordshire, Ron Pigram, Shire Publications, 1985.
3. Footpath Walks in Mid Herts. for Motorists, vols. 1,2,3, Mid Herts. Footpaths Soc., 1986.
4. Hertfordshire Chain Walk, East Herts. Footpaths Society, Castlemead Publications, 1987.
5. Hertfordshire Rambles, Liz Moynihan, Countryside Books, 1988.
6. Local Walks, South Beds., North Chilterns, Vaughan Basham, Book Castle, 1988.
7. Pub Walks in Hertfordshire, Alan Charles, Countryside Books 1994.
8. The Hertfordshire Way, Bert Richardson, Castlemead Publications, 1998.
9. Walks Herts. and Bucks., David Perrott, Laurence Main, Bartholomew, 1990.
10. Walks for Motorists, Chilterns Northern Area, Nicholas Moon, Frederick Warne, 1982.
11. Walks in Dacorum, Dacorum Borough Council, 1986.
12. Walks in Hertfordshire, Frank Dawes, Spurbooks Ltd, 1975.
13. Walks in the Hertfordshire Chilterns, Nicholas Moon, Shire Publications, 1986.
14. 24 Footpath Walks in Hertfordshire, Bill Frost, St Albans and District Footpaths Society, 1992.

WALKS LEAFLETS

15. Upper Lea Valley Through Walk, Upper Lea Valley Liaison Group, Herts. County Council.
16. Ver/Colne Valley Walk, County Planning Department, Herts. County Council.
17. Healthy Herts. Walks, Countryside Management Service, Herts. County Council.

NOTES

Admin Press Ltd, Tel: 01923 222444